Vegetarian Cooking

On a

Budget

Delicious, (mostly) healthy, and affordable

By

Lynette Spencer

Part of the Series: Budget-Friendly Living

Copyright Page

Vegetarian Cooking on a Budget: delicious, (mostly) healthy, and affordable

Copyright© 2019: Lynette Spencer of Write Useful

ISBN: 9781092769099

Independently published by Write Useful
Printed in the United States of America
First Edition published April 2019
Cover Design by Rebecacovers
Editing by J. Traveler Pelton
Books> nonfiction>culinary

Table of Contents

Introduction

I like food. I like how it tastes. I like how it smells. I like preparing it. I like when my pantry is full and I have many choices as to what to prepare. I like growing food in the summer, and choosing food at the store and the farmer's market. I like trying new foods and new recipes, and I like repeating recipes that loved ones have told me they like. I like sharing what I've made and feeding people.

I've noticed that what I eat has an effect on my temperament, mood, and health. If I eat too much junk food, it starts to bring me down into a grey depression, especially if I pair it with not exercising and not creating. If I eat too much sweetness and processed food and not enough whole foods and healthy foods, I get sick more often and it takes longer to get well. And it's not just me; what you eat is proven in much research and experience to have an effect on your health.

It's important to have balanced nutrition, but a lot of people think that is impossible to do while being on a tight budget. Supposedly the highly processed and junk foods are what is the most affordable – boxed macaroni and powdered not-actually-cheese, cheap white bread, super sugary jam, prepackaged cakes, etc. This is not true. It's very possible to eat well while keeping your food budget down and your food healthy.

In general, the closer you are to the food's natural state, the better the nutrition is. You don't have to take it too far by never heating food or using ready-made foods, but the nutrition in whole grains is better than that in bleached grains, the value in actual cheese is better than in highly processed cheese-like powders or chunks, the value in actual fruit is better than in fruit cocktails or fruity bits that are actually mostly corn syrup. One of the best tips for keeping you diet healthy is to read labels; you'll be surprised how often the blueberries in blueberry muffins are actually flavored chunks of gelatin instead of fruit.

Practice moderation, and avoid food that has too much sugar, oils, and salts. Don't eliminate them – your body needs foods with these nutrients. Most recipes will have some. A few of the recipes in this book have a lot; moderation doesn't mean never eat cookies. And if you bake them at home, you can use less sugar, or sneak in healthy mix-ins. Highly processed foods use additives, artificial flavorings, and chemical preservatives. They'll often substitute ingredients for cheaper, but less nutritious ingredients, or to suit popular buzzwords; the marketing will spin it to sound good, but the labels are required give the truth. For instance, "low fat" foods usually have a lot more sugar, and artificial flavorings are used instead of nutritious ingredients (remember the gelatin that's not really blueberries?).

Cooking on your own gives you more control of what's in your food. That doesn't mean you never used prepared foods, or ready-made kits, or frozen pizza, or sweets. It means balance. If you're using non-whole grain pasta, be sure the sauce and side dishes are nutritious.

Cooking vegetarian food (or any other healthy diet) also doesn't have to be expensive. If you go into a trendy all-natural health food store, you might come out with the idea that there's no way you can eat both healthfully and cheaply. Your whole month's grocery budget wouldn't buy two bags of groceries there, and you might feel like giving up just from looking around. Don't give up. That is far from the only place to get healthy food; those kind of stores can be fun to explore, but they are actually one of the most expensive places to do so. I'll discuss more detail on how to find affordable foods in the chapter on stocking your kitchen.

You can, by planning and shopping wisely, eat well and stay within budget. While there are some exceptions to rules, in general, following these guidelines will help keep your nutrition good and budget healthy.

The recipes often include tips, ideas for variations, and suggestions to try that might also expand your general kitchen skills.

This book also has information about how to set up your kitchen, what tools and supplies you need, how to stock your pantry, basic nutrition, seasonings, and how to shop for food in a budget-wise way.

Simple Guidelines: Tips for eating healthfully

There are a lot of books, YouTube channels, apps, guidelines, and clubs that can tell you in detail the hows and whys of many kinds of healthy diet. This can make you feel like eating well is complicated, confusing, contradictory, and just too hard. It doesn't have to be that way. While you can go into a ton of detail and micromanage your diet, here are some some simple guidelines that will help you keep generally on the right path.

Less processed is better. Over-processing is the way modern food companies break down food into less nutritious, but more shipping-friendly and shelf-stable foods. Doing this strips away nutrients. The manufacturer adds some back in, but it doesn't replace anywhere near what's been taken out, and adds in all kinds of artificial things that might negatively affect your body.

Consider bread, a very basic food that's a significant part of most people's diet. I baked homemade bread. It's tasty, nutritious, and inexpensive. I bought some bread, not much more cost. The homemade bread I didn't use went stale and got mold in a week because I didn't store it right. (If I'd frozen half the loaf to thaw out later, there would have been no loss for human consumption. My chickens loved it, though, so it wasn't a total waste.) The store bought bread never went moldy. It dried out, but had a high enough chemical count that nature couldn't get a toehold. Imagine what that does in your insides – how hard is it for your digestive system to break down something that resists nature like that?

Eat the rainbow. Eat different colored fruits and vegetables; the colors are related to the nutritive content. Keep multiple colors in your daily diet – leafy greens, orange carrots or squash, red berries, and so on. Have fruits and vegetables at every meal, and have your snacks, if you eat snacks, be fruits, vegetables, or whole grains. This doesn't have to be expensive; shop carefully, get canned, frozen, out of date but not spoiled, and seasonal produce. Keep a varied and colorful diet; this will help ensure you have complete nutrition. You'll need to keep an eye on a few things to be sure you get enough; these aren't all in need of special attention because of the vegetarian diet. More omnivorous people also need to be careful of their nutrition.

Often, when you're thinking about eating more vegetarian, or talking about being a vegetarian, people will ask you, "But where will you get your protein?" It's not hard at all to get enough protein on a vegetarian, or even vegan, diet. A diet that includes a variety of whole grains and legumes will provide the protein your body needs. If you also eat eggs and dairy, you'll have no problem at all keeping your protein intake adequate. But most vegetable based foods provide some protein; legumes have the most, fruits have the least. Peanut butter's a great source of protein (read labels to choose one that's lower in sugar and additives), as are beans, brown rice, vegetables. Eat a variety of grains, legumes, and nuts to get a complete range of nutrition.

Be aware that some nutrients you'll need to be especially conscious of including in your diet. They're not as readily available, and if you fall into a habit of eating the same few foods each day, you could find yourself deficient. Keep an eye out for sources of vitamin D, vitamin B-12, calcium, iron and zinc – these can be a little harder to find, especially if you're going vegan.

Vitamin D helps your body absorb calcium; without it, even if you have plenty of calcium intake, your body can't use it for your bones. The best way to get vitamin D is to spend time exposing your skin to direct sunlight, say 15 minutes or so 3-4 times a week; you body metabolizes it automatically. As people spend more and more time indoors, we see a lot of people with a vitamin D deficiency. How long you need to spend in the sun depends on the time of day and year (you need longer in winter than summer, and mid day is more effective than evening), amount of skin exposed (more skin equals more vitamin D – don't go overboard here, and get frostbite or indecency citations), where you are located on the globe (the closer to the equator, the more effective the sunlight), and how dark your skin is (darker skin protects you from the sun, but slows creation of vitamin). You can also find vitamin D in dairy and eggs.

Vitamin B-12 can be found in dairy products and eggs; proponents of organic food say that there are higher levels in organic foods. If you're looking more for vegan sources, it's also found in nutritional yeast and shiitake mushrooms. You might find it easiest to take a vitamin supplement or multivitamin to be sure you get enough B-12, if you don't feel like gorging on mushrooms.

Calcium builds strong bones and is important for your nervous system's health. It is most often identified with dairy products – and they are an excellent source. But they're far from the only source, and many excellent sources of calcium are plant-based. Calcium is also found in dark green vegetables (like kale and broccoli), black beans, butternut squash, and tofu.

Be sure to eat enough iron; it's important for your blood and therefore, all the rest of your body. Iron is a vital part of red blood cells, which carry oxygen throughout your body. If you're low on iron, you'll be fatigued all the time and get tired and out of breath very easily, even if you're in good shape. Vegetarians need to eat almost twice as much iron as more omnivorous people, as iron that come from plant sources instead of from eating blood metabolizes differently. You'll hear well-meaning advice that iron is only provided in meats, due to the blood content. That's not true, and iron is easy enough to find –

legumes, seeds, vegetables, and whole grains all have it. Even just cooking in cast iron pans can increase your iron intake significantly; I tend toward being anemic, and used to get dizzy and lightheaded often, but I haven't had any issues at all since I started cooking in cast iron.

Zinc helps you keep a healthy immune system; a lot of people only take zinc when they get sick and suck on zinc-fortified cough drops. But you'll get sick less often if you eat enough zinc in the first place. Zinc can be found in dairy products, nuts, and legumes. Cashews, chickpeas, soy based foods, and yogurt are good sources.

Omega 3 fatty acids help with heart health. They are found in eggs, walnuts, flaxseed and flaxseed oil, canola oil, and soy beans.

Iodine supports your metabolism; it is essential for a healthy thyroid. If you have a severe deficiency, you could get goiters. It's also vital for healthy pregnancies; lack of iodine can cause serious issues for the baby. Be sure to use iodized salt to be sure you're getting enough iodine. It's also found in seaweed, like that used to wrap around sushi.

Keep it whole. Eat whole grains and legumes. Legumes are dried beans, peas, soybeans, chickpeas, and lentils. They are great sources of protein, fiber, B-vitamins, iron, and phytonutrients. Whole grains provide fiber, protein, and a variety of vitamins and nutrients.

A lot of recipes include flour; you can use whole grain for all or part of it. For some recipes, like making a roux, whole grains will change the flavor of the food, or it might not work as well. Whole grains have more flavor of their own, and are heartier; some recipes that are more delicate may need to stick with white flour. Most things – quick breads, slow breads, pie crusts – you can use half or all whole wheat flour. Try adding rolled oats or barley to bread. Eat multigrain hot cereals, instead of sticking with instant oatmeal and cream of wheat.

Plan ahead. If you first get hungry and *then* try to plan dinner, you'll be more impulsive and tend to eat less healthfully (hungry bodies crave fats and sugars for a quick fix, instead of balance) and impulse spend or impulse eat (I don't have time or energy to plan a meal and cook, I'm ordering pizza/just making up this fast mac & cheese/grabbing some chips). If you've got it all planned out that you're making cornbread and beans for dinner – the beans are already in the slow cooker and will be right there, ready when you get home – it's easier to stick with your plan then to try to make a new one. You can also use this planning to talk yourself into staying healthier – no, I don't need fries, I've got chili waiting as soon as I get home.

Planning ahead also helps reduce waste. One major way to keep your food costs down is to stop throwing away food – use it. Current stats are that the average U.S. family throws away well over two thousand dollars worth of food a year. If you end up throwing away a large part of the food you buy, that does terrible things for your food budget. Remember my moldy bread? If I'd frozen the half loaf I didn't use at first, it would have been fine. Or if, after a couple days, I'd made it into bread pudding or a fritatta instead of letting it sit, ignored, on the shelf. It wasn't wasted – as it's all natural, I just gave it to my chickens, who loved it anyway – but still, I'd had other possibilities, and you might not have chickens. When you have leftovers, plan what to do – freeze them, pack them into smaller containers to take for lunches, or right then that you're making burritos from the leftover beans for dinner tomorrow.

Planning ahead helps you save money when you are shopping. Have an idea what's in season; that will help you get the most nutritious and least expensive fresh foods. Scan the sales pages of local groceries and see what's on sale. Know roughly what you plan to eat that week and make a list of what you need. Stick to your list and keep down impulse buys; I find that if I don't have a list, I tend to come out with several bags of groceries that I don't really need right now. If you want a little leeway in shopping, allot a certain amount of money for extras – things that are on clearance, a new food to try, that thing you forgot when you made your list. Don't go over that amount; that gives you both wiggle room and structure.

Read labels. Be aware of what you're buying and getting ready to put in your body. Sugar, artificial everything, and more sugars, hidden under other names, sneak into many prepared foods. Read the labels – do you really want pasta sauce that has a ton of added sugar, or bread that has nine ingredients you can't pronounce? You can watch for ingredients you've decided to avoid; a lot of people decide to avoid or limit consumption of monosodium glutimate, or high fructose corn syrup (a more processed version of simple corn syrup), or artificial sweeteners, or specific artificial colors. Reading labels and using them to make deliberate decisions gives you control over what you eat.

Reading labels also helps you keep to whatever type of vegetarianism you're choosing; some pasta sauces and salad dressings have anchovies, for instance; fine if you are a pescatarian; to be avoided if you're not. Some brands of canned refried beans use lard instead of vegetable oils. Know what you want and read to see if the food matches. After a while, this will become easy; you'll have learned what foods or companies fit what you want to have in your daily food and be able to shop quickly and efficiently.

Don't get empty. Unless you are doing a planned, short fast for religious or health reasons, don't let yourself get too hungry. I'm not talking eating half a dozen full meals, but have an apple and a cup of milk, or a handful to carrot sticks, or a small bowl of rice with raisins, especially before you go grocery shopping. If you're hungry, you're more likely to impulsively run through a drive through, or buy a lot of things you don't need but which called to your unconscious instinct of, "must get food now! going to starve!" When your body registers too low a food level, it starts craving fats and sugars for quick energy.

Drink water. Lots of water. Keep yourself hydrated. It's estimated that up to 75% of Americans are some level of dehydrated. Dehydration can cause problems including weight gain, foggy thinking, irritability, fatigue, kidney stones, joint pain, and dry skin. Severe dehydration can cause seizures, shock, kidney failure, and death.

Stomachs aren't too intelligent – sometimes when we feel like we're hungry, it's actually water we need. If you are planning enough food into your meals (keep a record for a few days and check, or use a food-tracking app – do not go below healthy requirements, eating disorders are NOT the goal) and still feel hungry, first drink a large glass of water and wait 15 minutes. If you're still hungry, then eat something. You're resetting your brain for healthy instincts.

Instead of drinking sodas or sweet drinks, drink water. In the US, tap water in most places is safe and free.

Good teas (or tisanes, since technically tea is only the leaves from one kind of bush and all the other hot drinks are tisanes) help you hydrate too. Don't add a lot of sugar to them, and they're great for your body.

Know why you are choosing this. Why are you a vegetarian, or considering eating more vegetarian dishes?

There are a lot of reasons to consider vegetarianism – economics (personal and widespread), health, ethics, religion. Vegetarianism can be less expensive; beans, seasonal fruits and vegetables, grains cost less than meat. If they're grown reasonably locally, they're better on the environment. (Shipping foods overseas kind of removes any positive environmental effect thanks to the shipping pollution.) Plant-based and lacto-ovo vegetarian food production does take much less water, land, and energy than what is required to grow cows for meat; whether it does for other kinds of animals is being debated by various environmental scientists. (If environmental effect is important to you, look at getting what you can from local producers to reduce shipping impact.)

Vegetarianism is more efficient as far as food production. For instance, you can grow between 24,000 and 60,000 pounds of potatoes on one acre; an acre will average out to 500 pounds of beef. Now, that's not an exact comparison – you can't keep a cow on 1 acre; they need a range, and can live on ground that's not suited for growing potatoes. It still averages out to a primarily plant-based diet being more efficient and better for the environment.

Years of research have thoroughly documents that vegetarianism is healthier lifestyle, if practiced well. (Technically eating nothing but potato chips and soda is vegetarian, but that is not healthy. Be sensible.) Cutting out most or all meat, keeping egg and cheese use moderate to low (or gone), and eating a well-balanced diet of healthy plant-based foods lowers blood pressure, lowers bad cholesterol, significantly decreases risk of heart attack and stroke, lowers risk of cancer, and can lower risk of Type 2 diabetes (a vegetarian diet can help manage diabetes if you have it). Many people feel more alert and energetic upon changing their diet to be more plant-based, including more whole foods – that is, as long as it's well balanced.

There are a lot of people who become vegetarian or vegan for ethical reasons. They learn about the conditions under which food animals are kept, and can't live with reinforcing that system. Or they don't believe other creatures should die so they can eat the poor animal's flesh. Many people view vegetarianism as a less selfish way to sustain themselves.

Some religions or individual practitioners of religions practice vegetarianism as part of their faith.

Vegetarianism, planned and practiced well, is balanced, healthy, and delicious.

There are different kinds of vegetarianism, with differing degrees of restrictiveness.

Vegans don't eat any animal-based products at all. No meat is obvious, but they also eat no eggs, no dairy, no honey, only plant-based gelatins, and most won't wear clothing that comes from animals as well (leather, wool, silk).

Lacto-vegetarians don't eat meat or eggs, but they do eat milk, cheese, butter, yogurt, and other dairy products.

Ovo-vegetarians don't eat meat or dairy, but do eat eggs.

Lacto-ovo vegetarians don't eat meat, but do eat eggs and dairy products. A lot of the recipes in this book are lacto-ovo vegetarian, but there are substitutions you can make if you don't want the eggs or dairy.

Pescatarians (or pesco-vegetarians) eat fish and seafood. Many of the stricter vegetarians are skeptical about this and of the next group.

Pollo-vegetarians (or **pollotarians**), who only eat chicken as a meat.

There are a lot of partial vegetarians, or mostly vegetarians. I have friends who are mostly vegan, but every few years they'll go backpacking in a really remote area where the water is clean and will eat fish that they catch as they're canoeing along. My husband is mostly a lacto-ovo vegetarian with me, but he will eat some of the meat he collects when hunting with his family (hunting season is a big event for them), or when fishing. He's a 95% vegetarian, only eats healthy meats he hunts, catches, or grows himself (but if he raises an animal, he gets attached and can't eat it.) Many, many people now are trying to keep their meat intake moderate, for a variety of reasons.

It's up to you how fully you embrace vegetarianism as a lifestyle, but consider these recipes as a useful introduction if it's new to you, or as a tasty addition if you've been eating this way for a while.

Side Dishes – Vegetables and so on

Vegetables are a huge part of what you eat when you start to eat more healthfully, whether you're a complete vegetarian, or just having more vegetarian meals and trying overall to be healthier. They are high in fiber, protein, vitamins, minerals, and micronutrients. They are a major part of keeping yourself and your diet healthy and well-balanced.

They're also a food that is often poorly prepared and vilified: overcooked, over-salted, soggy, bitter, unseasoned vegetables have turned many people off them. Most people will have a couple they don't like, but if you prepare them well and actually taste them, you might be surprised how delicious some of the veggies you'd mentally categorized as "icky" or "eat for duty but blech" are.

I was a picky, picky child and wouldn't eat a lot of things that I relish now. Brussels sprouts, fresh green beans, salsa, onions, peas – the list went on. Eventually as I grew up, I started tasting them, trying different preparations. And almost everything has multiple ways of deliciousness, even when some methods of preparation are still – can we say less than preferred?

Even if you think you don't like vegetables – prepare them well, try them a couple different ways, and be prepared to be pleasantly surprised.

How to Steam Vegetables

This is useful for most kinds of fresh and frozen vegetables you'll use as a side dish: broccoli, green beans, corn, cauliflower, peas, carrots, whatever. Canned vegetables are already cooked and only need to be heated up.

First Method:

This is the easiest one, as it only requires a regular pan and a stove.

Put 1 inch of water in pan and bring to boil, lower heat. Put vegetables in pan and cover tightly. Steam until veggies are as tender as you want. Time will vary, depending on kind of vegetable and how well done you want them; broccoli florets might only take 5 minutes, while carrots could take twenty or so. I like vegetables to be crisp-tender – cooked through but still firm. Poke with a fork to see if they're soft enough. Be careful about over cooking; some vegetables, like broccoli or spinach, get a bitter or sour taste when they're cooked too long.

Second Method:

Put veggies in a microwave-safe bowl with half an inch of water. Microwave on high, a minute at a time, stirring and turning the bowl between (very important; the microwave will scorch some parts and leave other frozen without stirring and turning) and checking tenderness until they reach desired degree of softness.

Third Method:

Set up a double-boiler with the steam top, or use a regular pan of water with a heat-safe sieve. Bring the water to a boil and put the vegetables in the top pan. Cover tightly and allow steam to cook veggies; check for done-ness by poking with a fork.

Now onto the recipes to get started!

Multiple Ways to Make Baked Potatoes

Potatoes are a vegetable; there are many ways to prepare them, some more healthy than others. Potatoes properly prepared, not overdoing the fat by deep-frying or drowning in butter, are nutritious. They contain potassium, vitamin B$_6$, vitamin C, and iron. If you eat them with the skin (wash them very well), they are high in fiber. A medium size, plain baked potato has only 110 calories. Most of the reason we think of potatoes as not healthy is because we cook them with a ton of oil, salt, butter, and cheese. Not that you can't use some of those; they do taste good, but be aware of how much you're adding.

While you can bake any potato; russets are the best; they are high-starch and get soft and fluffy when baked.

Method 1 – Open Oven Bake

Preheat your oven to 350.

First, wash your potatoes very well, especially if you're eating the skin. Scrub it thoroughly. Cut out eyes or suspicious-looking spots.

Poke the potatoes several times with a fork or knife. This isn't as important if you've had eyes to cut out, because what you're doing is adding ventilation. Potatoes make steam inside when they bake; if there's not a place for the steam to escape, they can blow up on you. That is not an exaggeration; they can explode, like a piece of popcorn, but with a lot more mess.

You can just put it in the oven here, but the next steps make it tastier.

Rub them all over with oil – olive oil tastes best, but any you can use any cooking oil, then with salt.

Put them on a cookie tray and put them in the oven. (You can just put them on the rack, but that makes rack-marks, and they can be tricky to get out then; if they roll away, you can burn yourself trying to get them)

Bake for an hour or so, or until soft. You check them by poking them with a skewer, fork, or knife. Do check before you pull them out; cooking time will vary based on the size of your potatoes – larger ones will take longer, smaller ones will take less time.

This gives you a crisp, tasty skin on the outside of the potato, and a fluffy, dryer inside.

Method 2 – Wrapped in Foil

Preparation is the same up until just before you put them in the oven. Wrap them well in foil before you put them on the cookie sheet.

This makes a softer skin and moister inside. The potatoes will stay hot longer if they are wrapped up in foil then if they are not, so if you are going to have a while before you get to eat them, this might be the best method. It's also the best method if you're cooking them in a fire while camping. Otherwise, the Idaho Potato Commission recommends not baking wrapped in foil – unwrapped potatoes bake faster, taste better in most taste tests, have less waste, and are faster to prepare since you don't have to take time to wrap them up.

Method 3 – Use the Microwave

Wash, clean, and ventilate the potatoes.

For a large potato, put in microwave and microwave on high for 5 minutes, turn it over, then microwave another 5 minutes. Use less time for a smaller potato. Some microwaves have a button that just says "potato"; you just push however many potatoes you have, and hit go.

These potatoes will not have a crispy skin; it will be soft.

This method is best if you're only baking a couple potatoes; microwaves will only hold a few at a time, and cooking time increases for each extra potato in the microwave.

Method 4 – In the Slow Cooker

Wash, clean, and ventilate the potatoes.

Rub with oil and salt.

Put in the slow cooker and cook on high until they're done, 3-5 hours. Check after 2 1/2 or 3 hours; cook longer if needed. Once you know how long your slow cooker takes (I have 2, and they take different amounts of time. One is old.), you'll be able to plan better for next time.

However you bake them, serve them hot with desired toppings. Try butter, sour cream, chives, chopped broccoli, gravy, cheese, or non-bacon bits.

Mashed Potatoes

Mashed potatoes are a popular food at family dinners; they're one of my husband's favorites and he'd like to eat them more often than I make them.

8-10 potatoes

1 stick butter

1/2 cup milk

Salt and pepper to taste

Wash and peel the potatoes and cut them into 1-inch cubes. Rinse the cubes.

Bring a large pan of water to boil. There needs to be enough water to cover the potatoes completely. Add the potatoes – carefully, don't splash yourself. Boil them until the are soft when you poke a fork in them. While boiling, I like to skim off the starch bubbles that form on the surface; this is not necessary.

Drain the potatoes.

Put potatoes, butter, salt and pepper in a bowl and mash them together. This is easiest with an electric mixer, but you can do it with a hand-held potato masher if you don't have a mixer.

Add the milk by splashes until the potatoes reach the consistency you want. Be careful; too much, and they get runny.

Serve.

Twice Baked Potatoes

This recipe has a lot more oil than plain baked potatoes, but it is delicious. And you can see that an appetizer that would cost you 8$ in a restaurant or so can be made at home for much less.

4 baked potatoes – whichever method you like.

4 T melted butter/olive oil (I go half of each, melt butter and mix them together. You can add garlic or other seasonings to this if desired.)

Salt to taste

1 cup shredded cheddar cheese (can use other cheese if you'd rather; Colby-Jack is also good.)

8 T sour cream

Other toppings if desired: vegan bacon bits, chives, chopped and cooked broccoli

Preheat oven to 400 and lightly oil a cookie sheet.

Cut baked potatoes in half lengthwise. Scoop out the insides with a spoon, leaving about 1/3 to 1/2 inch in skin. Put the scooped innards in a storage container and refrigerate to use to make another dish later. (Mix in mashed potatoes, potato soup, colcannon bake, or just heat up and eat.)

Brush oil/butter mix all over the inside and outside of the potatoes. Lay open side down on the cookie sheet. Sprinkle skins with salt, if you wish.

Bake for 10-15 minutes. Take out of oven and turn over, open side up. Be careful, they're hot. Sprinkle with salt and pepper to taste.

Brush with some more of the butter/oil mix, if it's not all used up. Put back in oven and bake 10-15 minutes, until starting to turn golden brown.

Take out of oven. Put 1-2 T of cheese in potato skins, spreading around so it covers surface.

Put back in oven and bake 5-10 minutes or so, until cheese is melted and bubbly.

Take out of oven. Put 1 T sour cream in each skin. Sprinkle with other toppings. Serve.

Actually Tasty Brussels Sprouts

I dislike Brussels sprouts, or at least I thought I did. I thought they were icky and bitter. Turns out I'd never had them prepared the right way for me.

You'll need a cast iron pan for this. You could use a regular baking dish if you haven't had luck finding reasonably priced cast iron yet, but I find cast iron works best.

1 package or stem fresh Brussels sprouts.

2-4 T olive oil

1-3 cloves fresh garlic, chopped or pushed through a garlic press (depends on taste and size of cloves. You can use 1/2 tsp garlic powder instead)

1/4 cup fresh Parmesan cheese (You can use the kind in the shaker can, but fresh tastes better. You can use more if you want.)

Salt and Pepper

Preheat oven to 400.

Coat pan thoroughly with oil.

Slice off stem end of sprouts, then cut the sprouts in half length-wise, unless they are very small.

Toss (carefully; they might come apart) with olive oil, garlic, a few pinches of salt, and pepper.

Lay sprouts in pan face-down.

Bake for 35 minutes, or until they are golden brown. About 5 minutes before you remove them from oven, sprinkle with Parmesan and return to oven for cheese to melt. If you are vegan, you can skip the cheese.

You can add a sliced red onion to the vegetables when you are tossing them in oil for a change of flavor.

Zucchini Patties

2 medium zucchini, grated

1/2 tsp salt

1/2 chopped onion

2 eggs, beaten

1 T chopped fresh basil, or 1 tsp dried.

Dried bread crumbs, about a cup.

Oil for frying

Mix zucchini and salt. Let stand for 10 minutes. Squeeze the zucchini well to get rid of excess fluid. A good way to do this is to gather it up into a clean tea towel and squeeze that very hard; you can twist the towel for a little extra tension.

Stir together zucchini, onion, eggs, and spices. Add bread crumbs, a little at a time, until it all starts to stick together.

Heat oil in a skillet. Drop mixture into the hot oil by large spoonfuls and flatten a bit with the back of the spoon. Cook until crisp and golden on each side.

This is a basic recipe; you can try different seasonings and add-ins. Try tarragon instead of basil. Add some cottage cheese, or top with sour cream and chives.

You can also line a cookie sheet with parchment paper, drop patties on that, brush lightly with oil, and bake at 350. They'll be a lot dryer, but less oily.

No-Crab Crabcakes

Another zucchini pancake! I've had some non-vegetarian friends over for dinner, and they said it tasted just like delicious crabcakes. Then they went back for seconds and thirds and took leftovers home with them. (I'd made a really big batch.) They are delicious as-is, as a side dish. They also make good sandwich patties – bread, butter, and "crab" cakes is delicious.

2 cups grated zucchini

1/4 cup finely chopped onion

1 cup dried breadcrumbs

2 large eggs

1 tsp Old Bay seasoning.

1 ½ T mayonnaise OR 1 ½ T melted butter

1/4 cup flour for dredging.

About a half cup oil for frying

Squeeze excess fluid from zucchini. Doesn't have to be bone-dry, but not soggy.

Mix everything except the flour and frying oil together thoroughly. You can use a large spoon, but squishing it together with your hands is easier.

Form mixture into patties. Dredge patties in flour. (To dredge, put flour in a bowl and roll patties in it till they are covered in a light coat of flour.)

Heat oil over medium-high heat. Fry patties until golden brown. Put on plate with paper towel for soaking up excess oil. Handle patties gently; they are crumbly.

Roast Root Vegetables (or cauliflower)

The most common veggie I do this with is potatoes. However, carrots, parsnips, beets, turnips, and other root veggies can all get this treatment. You can do this is cauliflower as well. It won't need to bake quite as long, but is delicious oven roasted. I like to mix several together; one vegetable blend I like to make pretty often (especially as a side dish to cottage cheese loaf) is potatoes, carrots, and parsnips. I'll write this recipe for potatoes; the other root veggies need to cook for about the same length of time.

4 potatoes (Or 2 potatoes, a carrot, and a parsnip, etc.)

2-3 T oil (I like to use olive oil, but unless you find it on sale or in a bent and dent, it's not the cheapest. Use what you have.)

Seasoning Blend – premade or your own.

Preheat oven to 400. Grease a cookie sheet.

Wash the vegetables thoroughly. Peel them if you don't want the peels; I usually leave them on if they're not tough.

Slice as desired. If I want french fries, I'll cut the potatoes into long slices. Otherwise, I cut them into about 1 inch cubes.

Rinse and put in a mixing bowl.

Sprinkle the oil over the potatoes. Shake the spice blend over them and toss together until spices are spread evenly across the potatoes. I often find that once tossed, I don't have as much spice as I thought, and add more and toss again.

Spread evenly across cookie sheet and bake in oven until your desired degree of done-ness; turn every 15-20 minutes. My husband is fine with eating them as soon as they soft all the way through and slightly browned, and I like to bake them till they're kind of crispy.

For seasoning blends, I switch it up to match whatever I'm having the roast veggies with. I have several flavors of Mrs. Dash's, Italian spice blend, jerked seasoning blend, lemon pepper, Cajun spice, seasoned salt, just salt and pepper, and curry blends. They're not all for this recipe – I use them in different things. You can use any seasonings you want on your roast veggies.

Roast Asparagus (or any other veggie)

I love asparagus in spring. We had a big patch of it in the garden when I was a kid, and it was the first thing ready to eat every year, so to me, it tastes like spring and warmth and getting to be outside. You want to be careful not to overcook asparagus; canned asparagus always tastes sad and overdone to me.

You can eat fresh asparagus raw, or prepare it with a basic steam-cooking as described at the start of this chapter. You can also do other things with it, like this.

1 handful of fresh asparagus stalks

1-2 T oil, olive preferably

Salt and pepper to taste

Lemon juice

Preheat oven to 425. Lightly oil a cooking sheet or a cast-iron pan.

Wash the asparagus and snap of any woody ends.

Toss carefully with the olive oil.

Lay in a single layer in your baking dish, and bake for 12-15 minutes, until just tender.

Sprinkle with lemon juice just before serving, or serve with a slice of lemon so people can do it themselves.

There are a lot of ways to switch up seasonings. I really like adding a crushed clove of garlic (or three) to the olive oil and asparagus when I'm tossing it. You can also add parmesan cheese, either when mixing at beginning, or sprinkled over for the last 4 minutes of roasting.

Try it with other herbs; tarragon and rosemary are good.

Asparagus is also really good with hollandaise sauce; there's a recipe for that in the chapter on sauces. Roast it or steam it, and pour a little hollandaise over it just before serving.

You can use this method of preparation with almost any vegetable. You'll need to adjust the cooking time if they are denser; carrots take longer, half an hour or so; broccoli about the same and sliced or cubed squash somewhere in the middle.

Cheesy Broccoli

6 cups broccoli florets

2 T butter

2 T unbleached flour

1/4 tsp dry mustard powder

1 cup milk

1 ½ cups sharp cheddar cheese, grated

Salt and pepper to taste

Prepare cheese sauce first:

Make a roux by melting the butter over medium-low heat, then whisking in the flour and mustard powder and continuing to whisk until a light golden brown.

Whisk in the milk gradually, no more than a quarter cup at a time, stirring continually to be sure that roux and milk mix completely without lumps. (You can usually stir out any lumps that happen). Stir over med-low heat until sauce thickens.

Add the cheese, stirring until completely melted. Add salt and pepper as desired. Remove from heat.

Steam broccoli. You can start it steaming while you're making the cheese sauce; just be careful not to overcook. Remove from heat as soon as it's done.

Pour cheese sauce over the broccoli and serve at once.

You can use this cheese sauce with other vegetables; it's great with cauliflower. It's tasty over roast potatoes, or even over pasta. The cheese sauce recipe is repeated in the sauce chapter, with variations for different cheese and seasonings.

Cabbage Steaks

This is a tasty way to make cabbage. Any leftovers can be just reheated, or chopped and added to soup or a casserole, or used in a casserole. Cabbage is nutritious and inexpensive. For a small family or individual, one cabbage can be divided between several dishes or meals.

1 head cabbage

4 T olive oil
Salt and Pepper

Chopped garlic or dried garlic (optional)

Preheat oven to 375. Grease a baking sheet or line it with parchment paper.

Core cabbage. Then sit it with the bottom side down, and cut it into 1 inch thick slices (the "steaks"). If you don't need a whole cabbage worth, wrap the rest well and refrigerate till later.

Use pastry brush to brush oil on the cabbage steaks on both sides (carefully, they'll come apart if you're not careful) and lay them on baking sheet. You could also just drizzle on the oil; I find it easier to be consistent and thorough with a brush.

Season with salt and pepper, and garlic if desired. (If you're using dried garlic, be careful and go lightly – it's really concentrated.)

Cover with aluminum foil if desired – covering means moister cabbage, uncovered means it gets a little crispy around the edges. I like it slightly brown, so I don't usually cover it. You can carefully turn it halfway through, if you want.

Bake until cabbage is desired done-ness; test by poking with a fork. If it goes in easily, it's done. This usually takes between half an hour and 45 minutes.

Carrot Salad

Another dish there are multiple variations on. This one is kind of sweet, kind of tart, with raisins.

1 pound carrots

1 can pineapple bits (optional, but it's good)

1/2 cup raisins

1 cup warm water for soaking the raisins. (You could also use the juice off the pineapple when you drain it.)

1/2 cup mayonnaise

Soak the raisins in the warm water (or pineapple juice) so that they swell up and get soft. (You could skip this step; then you'd have chewy raisins. Soft seem to fit better here.) While raisins are soaking, prepare carrots.

Wash the carrots well. Shred them – you can do this by grating them by hand, or running through the grater setting of a food processor.

Drain the raisins. Put the drained raisins, carrots, and pineapple in a large bowl. Add the mayonnaise.

Mix well. Chill and serve.

Some people add a spoonful of sugar to sweeten this. Others add a spoonful of lemon juice to make it tart; you choose which or neither of these to do. You can also add a cup of (vegan if you're being careful to watch out for gelatin sources) mini marshmallows to make it sweet. Kids tend to really like that, but it makes it a lot less healthy.

Ambrosia

This isn't vegetables, but it is common salad at summer cookouts and potlucks around here. You can add all kinds of things to it; I'll talk about that after the main recipe.

1 can mandarin oranges, drained

1 can pineapple tidbits, drained

1 cup mini marshmallows (if you're careful about gelatin sources, get vegan ones)

1 cup dried, shredded, sweetened coconut

1 ½ cup whipped topping or whipped cream

Mix everything together in a bowl. Serve chilled. It's that easy.

Now, for variations.

You can use 1/2 to 1 cup sour cream mixed instead of whipped cream, if you want less sweet. Or substitute sour cream for part of the whipped topping, if you still want some sweetness. (Note that homemade whipped cream is not necessarily sweet, depending whether you add sugar or not.)

You can beat 1/2 to 1 package of room temperature cream cheese until it's fluffy and mix that with the whipped topping before you add it to the fruit.

You can add a cup or so of cottage cheese to everything else.

You can add half a cup of chopped nuts or sunflower seeds.

You can add all kids of other fruits – halved grapes, chopped apples, raisins, dried cranberries, maraschino cherries, sliced bananas, sliced strawberries, chopped peaches, and on and on. If you increase the fruit a lot, add more whipped topping and shredded coconut to keep the consistency and to have enough white fluffy goodness to coat everything thoroughly.

And to finish it all up, you can put a spoonful of granola of top of each serving.

Creamed Spinach

While I like spinach in salads, or steamed with a bit of salt and pepper, or with lemon juice, this is another tasty way to prepare it, and it might be more palatable for picky eaters. There are a lot of ways to make creamed spinach, but the basic ingredients of most of those are spinach, alliums, roux, dairy, nutmeg. Here's one possibility.

1/2 onion, chopped fine

2 cloves garlic, chopped or pressed

2 T butter

2 T flour

1 cup milk

1/4 cup Parmesan

1/4 tsp nutmeg

16-20 ounces chopped, frozen spinach, thawed and drained OR 2 bags baby spinach, washed and any hard stems clipped off.

Sauté the onion for a few minutes in the butter, then add the garlic and sauté till golden brown.

Add the flour and stir, then slowly mix in the milk and stir till thickened. Add Parmesan and nutmeg.

If you're using fresh spinach, chop it up a bit, then put it in a large pan that has a lid, along with a little water or oil, just so it doesn't stick. Steam lightly; it will drastically shrink in volume. Once hot and wilted, remove from heat and drain if it's really wet.

Mix creamy sauce with spinach and serve.

You can use cream, evaporated milk, heavy cream, cream cheese, sour cream – all kinds of dairy, based on what's in your cupboards.

Basic Cabbage

There are a lot of ways to use cabbage, but here is a basic, buttery sauté. You can use this to pre-cook it for casseroles or quick soups, or serve as a side dish.

1/2 cabbage, cut. I usually chop it into bite-sized pieces, but you can just slice it into wedges or slices if you want.

2 T butter

Water enough to steam, less than half a cup.

1 tsp salt

Melt the butter in a pan that has a lid; I usually use a frying pan that has a lid for ease of stirring (and because I love using my cast iron).

Put the cabbage in and add water and salt. Stir well, lower heat to low-med, and cover.

Cook until softened, about 15-20 minutes, stirring occasionally. If it looks like it's getting too dry and is apt to stick, add a little water. You don't want it soggy, and you do want most of the water to steam off. If you want it softer, you can cook it longer.

You can use a whole cabbage instead of half; I usually don't, because there are just two of us at home. But if you're going to use it in other recipes, like the next one, you might want to make the whole thing up. You'll need a bigger pan then.

Cabbage Casserole

This starts with cabbage that has just been cooked as described above, stopping while it's still firm.

4 cups chopped, cooked cabbage

1/2 onion, chopped

1 T butter

1/3 cup canned tomatoes, chopped (save the rest of the can for another recipe, maybe a pasta sauce or soup)

1 cup white sauce (described in chapter on sauces – roux and milk, with a little salt and pepper)

1/2 cup shredded cheddar cheese

1/2 cup bread crumbs or crushed crackers

Preheat oven to 350. Grease a 1 ½ quart casserole dish.

Sauté the onion in the butter; you can do it in the same pan in which you cooked the cabbage if you're doing this all at once.
Mix cabbage, tomatoes, onion, and white sauce.

Put into casserole dish and spread evenly.

Top with cheese and crumbs (you can mix them or layer them, whichever)

Bake for 25 minutes, without a lid, or until brown and bubbly.

Stuffed Cabbage Leaves

There are a lot of things you can stuff the leaves with; I'll put a few recipes down below.

To prepare cabbage leaves for stuffing, choose 6 or so large leaves – the outside leaves are good, maybe one or two leaves in so they aren't discolored. Wash them well and put them in a large bowl, laying flat. Boil a pan or teakettle of water, and pour it over the leaves in the bowl, covering them completely. Let it sit for ten minutes, then remove leaves, pat dry, and cut in half along center vein. Cut the stiff vein out of the leaves and stack them to the side, to use when your filling is ready.

Put 1-2 T of filling on one end of the leaf. Roll it up, tucking in the ends to make a neat package that is completely closed, and fasten shut with a toothpick. Then steam them over boiling water in the steaming attachment to a double boiler, or boil them in broth, for half an hour or until the cabbage leaves are soft.

Stuffing 1 – Spinach, Cheese, and Rice

1 cup frozen spinach, thawed and drained

1 egg

1 cup shredded cheese (cheddar is good)

1 tsp salt

1 tsp grated onion, or a small pinch onion powder.
1 cup cooked rice

Mix everything together thoroughly. Wrap in cabbage leaves and cook as described above.

Stuffing 2 – Lentil and Rice, with a sauce

2 cups cooked lentils

1 ½ cups cooked rice – brown rice is good, but use what you have

1 small onion, diced

1 T oil

1 T cider vinegar

Sauce:
2 T soy sauce

1 tsp paprika

1 large can tomato puree

1 ½ tsp cider vinegar

1 T brown sugar

Salt and pepper to taste

Preheat oven to 350 and grease a 9 inch square baking dish.

Sauté onion in oil in large pan. Add lentils, rice, 2 T vinegar, soy sauce, and paprika to the pan and mix together well, then remove from heat.

In a bowl, combine tomato puree, 1 ½ tsp vinegar, and brown sugar to make a sauce.

Put half a cup of the sauce in the bottom of the baking dish and spread evenly.

Wrap the lentil filling in the cabbage leaves as described, and lay them in the sauce in the pan.

Cover with the remaining sauce. Put lid on pan or cover with foil and bake for an hour.

Remove from oven, let stand 5 minutes, then serve.

Stuffing 3 – Cottage Cheese Loaf

Mix up a half-batch of cottage cheese loaf, as described in chapter on non-meats.

Roll up into cabbage leaves.

You can cook this by steaming, or by baking in a covered casserole dish, covered with gravy or with mushroom soup.

Stuffing 4 – Cheesy Potatoes

2 cups mashed potatoes. (You can microwave-bake 3 potatoes and scoop out the insides to use if you don't have leftover mashed potatoes)

1/2 onion, diced fine

1 clove garlic, chopped or pressed; or 1/8 tsp garlic powder (optional; I like garlic, onion alone is fine)

1 T oil or butter

1/2 to 1 cup cheese, shredded (you can use cottage cheese or feta – feta's strong, you might want a bit less if you use that)

1/4 cup vegetarian bacon bits, (optional) (most of the ones that don't actually say 'real bacon' are vegetable protein; check the label)

Sauté the onion in the oil until translucent; add the garlic and sauté another minute or two.

Add the potatoes to the pan and combine, until heated and thoroughly mixed. If it's too thick to mix, which might happen if you're using baked potato insides instead of mashed potatoes, you can add a little milk to thin it a bit.

Remove from heat and mix in cheese and non-bacon bits.

Roll up in cabbage leaves as directed. You can steam this, or cook in a lidded skillet with some vegetable broth and butter until cabbage leaves are tender.

You can basically roll up anything that goes okay with cabbage in a softened cabbage leaf and either steam it or cook it in a lidded pan with some kind of sauce or broth. They can make tasty dumplings in a soup or stew, or you can use them kind of like meatballs on top of pasta with a sauce, depending on the stuffing. Experiment! It will all be edible, though some will taste better than others.

Soups and Similar

Soup is simply a liquid dish that is made by cooking ingredients (vegetables, grains, legumes, seasonings) in some kind of fluid (water, broth, milk).

That basic definition should make it clear what a wide, wide range soup covers. Creamy potato soup? Clear broth? Lentil and potato? All soups. Soups can be made chilled for hot weather, or hot for cold weather. They're a comfort food when you're not feeling well. They're healthy, inexpensive, and can be made in such wide variety that they are rarely boring. Soups can be savory or sweet, creamy or clear, hearty or light.

You can eat them by themselves, but soups also go amazingly well with hot rolls, cornbread, flat bread, or sandwiches.

I'm including similarly cooked-in-liquid foods in this section. Rice and legumes are often themselves ingredients in soup, but that is not all. They are ingredients in recipes spread throughout this book (black bean burgers; curries and stir fries over rice, rice and raisins for breakfast). They are included in this chapter because they are cooked in water, or perhaps in broth for flavoring.

Cooking Beans

This is general directions of how to cook dried beans. You will use dried beans as ingredients to chili, as part of a soup, when making burritos, taco salad, or nachos, as a part of quite a few other recipes. While you can buy cans of cooked beans, it's cheaper to cook your own. A 15 ounce can of pinto beans and a 1 lb bag of dried beans costs about the same, but you only get 2 cups of beans with the can, you get at least 6 cups of beans with dried beans.

For a basic, no-frills bean preparation, you will need:

1 bag dried beans

2 T butter or oil

2 tsp salt

1 small to medium onion (optional, but I always use one)

Lots of water

First, rinse and pick over the beans. Make sure they are clean, and you've picked out any bad beans or stones. (I haven't found a stone in a while, but when I was a kid, beans always had at least a couple stones or dirt chunks; I think they've improved their processing practices.)

You can either soak the beans for 6 hours or overnight, or boil them for 10 minutes and then rinse them and change the water. This helps cut down on getting gas from eating the beans. It's not absolutely necessary for any beans except kidney beans. **Important**: if you are making kidney beans, _always_ boil them for 15 to 30 minutes and then rinse them; they can make you pretty sick if you don't. Rinsing and cooking thoroughly removes all risk, though. If you are cooking kidney beans in a slow cooker, do the boil-and-rinse before you transfer them into the slow cooker.

If you are using an onion (I recommend it), peel the onion and cut off the roots and top. You can chop it if you want, but I always just toss it in whole.

Next, put beans in the pan you'll cook them in and cover them with water; have the water cover the beans by at least 3 inches. Put in the butter, salt, and onion. Bring to a low boil and lower heat to medium. Cooking time varies depending on the kind of bean; a good estimate for most beans is about an hour to and hour and a half, longer for larger beans; they have to cook all the way through, after all

Beans are done when they are tender all the way through. A quick test for most beans is to lift a couple out in a spoon and blow on them; beans that are close to done or done will have their skin curl up and wrinkle, beans that are not done don't. If the skin wrinkles, let a bean cool enough that you won't get burnt and taste it. The beans should be tender all the way through, with no crunch or crispness.

Keep in mind that lentils and peas don't need soaked or precooked, and they cook fast, sometimes it only takes 15-20 minutes or so to cook lentils, while lima beans might need up to 4 hours.

Lentils and split peas can be cooked directly in soups; other beans need to be cooked first before being added to soup or having ingredients added to them to make soup.

You can cook beans in a slow cooker; for kidney beans especially, boil and rinse them before putting them in the cooker. Cover them at least 2 inches deep with water, cover the slow cooker, and cook for 3 to 6 hours.

Cooking Rice

This is included in this chapter for similar reasons as the beans. A lot of rice recipes will have you carefully balancing rice and water so that the water completely evaporates just as the rice finishes; I like to cook in extra water, and drain off the water, sometimes with an extra rinse. This will not work if you want sticky rice.

Rice

Oil (optional)
Salt

Water

Measure out how much rice you want; keep in mind it will double in volume. Rinse thoroughly.

Add half a teaspoon to a teaspoon of salt to a pan of water and bring the water to a boil; you can add a spoonful of oil if you want, but it's not necessary.

Add the rice and stir it. Bring the temperature down to a simmer for 15 to 20 minutes for white rice, or 45 minutes for brown rice.

Drain the rice through a sieve; I sometimes rinse it again, especially with brown rice. Return to pan, fluff with fork, and serve.

Grandma P's Corn Chowder

I have several recipes from her recipe box. This is a soup my paternal grandma served the first time I brought my then-fiance to visit, and he's talked about it ever since. The card is printed, and she wrote her own alterations on it, including the comment at the top, "Good". I'll include her additions in a coherent whole. She was vegan; you don't have to use soy milk, you can use regular milk, as described in the after-recipe notes.

3 cups water

2 cups diced potatoes

1 small onion chopped (or 2 tsp onion powder)

1/2 tsp celery seed (or 1/2 cup chopped celery
2 cups whole kernel corn

2 cups thick soy milk (2 cups water to 1 cup soy milk powder)

1 ½ tsp salt

3/4 T dried basil

1/2 block firm tofu, cubed and sautéed in olive oil (optional)

Combine 3 cups water, chopped potatoes, onion, celery, salt, and basil.

Simmer until the potatoes are tender, then add the corn and the soymilk.

Heat thoroughly until it thickens.

Add the tofu, if you are going to be using tofu.

This is a pretty inexpensive recipe, even with soymilk costing more than regular milk. (Be sure you're using unsweetened, unflavored soy milk powder; vanilla or hazelnut would taste awful!) If you want to use regular milk, there are a couple ways to do it. One is to use powdered milk the same way the recipe calls for soy milk powder. Another is to make a roux (equal parts oil or melted butter and flour, stirred together over low to medium heat for a few minutes), then stirred constantly while you mix in two cups of whole milk or one can of evaporated milk. The typical roux ratio is 2 T each butter and flour to one cup of liquid. This results in a gravy-like consistency; you won't want that for a soup, so for this whole pot, start with 4 T and see if that thickens it enough. Add to soup at appropriate point and finish recipe as directed.

As with all soups, you can switch this one up by adding other veggies. Try using a little garlic along with the onion. Chop in a carrot or some parsnips or some cauliflower.

Lentil and Rice Soup

This is a really cheap, nutritious, and delicious soup. This recipe came from some friends; my copy has notes about which family members like it and recipe changes she tried, like "try with cayenne pepper and garlic". (I like with garlic, but only light cayenne.)

8 cups water

1 cup dried lentils, rinsed and drained

1/2 cup brown rice, rinsed and drained

1 large onion, chopped

1/4 cup olive oil

salt and pepper

Combine water, lentils, and rice in a large pot, bring to a boil. Cover and reduce the heat; simmer for 1½ hours, until the lentils are very tender. If too much water evaporates away, add a little more.

Sauté the onion in the olive oil over very low heat for 30 to 60 minutes. (That is a long, long time, heat must be low so that onion carmelizes instead of burning.) Add to the soup, add salt and pepper, and simmer another 10 minutes or so.

This soup is great with fresh bread and butter.

If you don't have olive oil, you can use whatever oil you have, but watch the heat and it will not taste exactly the same.

Split Pea Soup

2 T olive oil (or the oil you have)

2 finely chopped celery stalks

2 medium leeks, white part only, chopped (If you don't have leeks, use an onion)

2 medium carrots, cleaned and sliced
4 oz non-meat bacon bits (read the labels; a lot of them are flavored soy protein)

1/2 tsp dried thyme

2 cloves garlic, minced

8 cups water

1 pound bag of split peas, rinsed and picked over

1 bay leaf

1/4 cup fresh chopped dill (or 1 T dry)

2 T soy sauce

1/2 to 1 tsp each salt and black pepper

In large cooking pot, heat oil over medium heat, then add carrots, leeks, and celery, sauté for 5 minutes, stirring often, until veggies starts to soften.

Add non-bacon, thyme, and garlic and stir for another 2 minutes.

Add water, peas, and bay leaf and stir. Bring to a simmer, cover, and cook for about 2 1/2 hours, until peas are soft.

Add soy sauce, salt, pepper, and dill after you remove from heat.

You can use 1/4 tsp of smoke flavoring instead of bacon bits. Sometimes I skip the dill entirely; to me it's a bit of an acquired taste and is rarely in my pantry.

You can use 1 tsp of celery seed instead of the celery. That does lower the vegetable content, as it's a spice instead of counting towards your vegetable intake; it has less fiber as well.

You can use garlic powder instead of cloves of garlic; 1/8 tsp of garlic powder for each clove replaced.

Vegetable Soup

This recipe has a ton of variations – use what vegetables you have on hand. Here's the basic recipe that you can work off of.

2 small onions or 1 large one, chopped

3 T oil

3 cloves garlic

2 quarts vegetable broth (or 2 quarts water and 4 cubes or tsp of bouillon)

3 sticks celery, chopped

3 carrots, chopped

2 large or 3-4 small potatoes, cubed

1 small cabbage, or half a large one, cored and chopped

1-2 cups green beans (frozen or a can, drained)

1-2 cups corn (frozen or a can, drained)

1 tsp salt

1 tsp pepper

In very large pot, sauté onions and garlic until translucent.

Add the broth. Bring to a boil and add the carrots and potatoes; simmer 15 minutes.

Add the rest of the vegetables. Simmer until carrots and potatoes are soft.

Serve.

Now, you can add pretty much any vegetable you have, or leave out ones you don't. Add them with their similarly dense compatriots – for example, add parsnips with the potatoes, as they need a longer cook time. Add kale, chopped tomatoes, or spinach with the cabbage and green beans, or even a little after, as they don't need as long.

Try adding cooked beans, either a can or leftovers from a bean dish. You can throw in a half cup of (rinsed and cleaned) lentils and/or barley when you add the broth.

Add some pasta; make alphabet soup, or put in a handful of macaroni. (Remember pasta swells and soaks up moisture; don't overdo it)

Add seasonings. I like to float a couple bay leaves and add parsley and/or rosemary. Try adding a teaspoon of chili pepper for some zing

Cabbage Soup

1 onion, chopped

2-3 T olive oil

2-5 cloves garlic, chopped.

2 quarts water

4 tsp vegetable bouillon grains, or 4 cubes vegetable bouillon
1 tsp salt

1/2 tsp pepper

1/2 head cabbage, chopped

1 can chopped tomatoes, drained

In a large cooking pot, sauté the onion in the oil until translucent; add garlic and sauté for another few minutes, until golden brown.

Put water in the pot; dissolve bouillon in it. Add onion and garlic, add salt and pepper. Bring to a boil.

Add cabbage and tomatoes. Simmer until cabbage is softened.

Serve with bread and butter.

Grandma B's Homemade Noodles

Grandma wasn't vegetarian, and would put these in chicken soup and in turkey broth every Thanksgiving. You can cook them and serve with butter and pepper, put them in almost any vegetable soup, put them in broths, serve with cheese – they are a good basic pasta.

1 egg, beaten well

1/2 tsp salt

1/2 tsp baking powder

1-1½ cups flour, depending how many you want to make

Around 2-3 T of milk, enough to make a dough

Mix it all together and knead it a couple minutes, until it's well blended and is a cohesive dough.

Then flour about half of your kitchen table and roll this dough out very thin.

Cut dough into strips with a sharp knife (or a pizza cutter – a modern invention useful for all kinds of cutting) and let it lie on the table to dry for two hours after cutting.

Carefully drop noodles into boiling broth. It makes a large pot of noodles and thickens the broth nicely.

Drop Dumplings

Another thing that's tasty to add to soups and stews is dumplings. This recipe is very similar to say, a biscuit recipe, but instead of baking it, you cook it directly in your soup. It's good with brothy soups, and doesn't seem to go quite as well with cream soups.

1 ½ cups flour

2 tsp baking powder

1 tsp salt

3 T butter, chopped into cubes

3/4 cup milk (you can use water if you don't have milk)

Sift dry ingredients together.

Crumble in the butter until it looks like find crumbs. You can do this in a food processor, or just squish it in your hands until it's well-blended.

Mix in the milk.

Drop by spoonfuls into boiling soup, broth, or stew. Cook at least 10 minutes, covered. (Time may vary, depending on how large your dumplings are.)

Great Grandma Moore's Depression Recipes

The next three soups (and some recipes in other sections) are handed from my mother's mother's mother. I've altered them a bit to make them vegetarian, but included the original recipe in parentheses.

GGM's Bean Soup

3 cups (1 ½ pounds) dried navy beans

1 can diced tomatoes, undrained

1 large onion, chopped

1 T olive oil or 1 T real butter (1 meaty ham hock or 1 cup diced cooked ham – which since they raised hogs, they had.)
A few drops of smoke flavoring, if desired
2 cups vegetable broth or chicken-like broth (Of course, Great-Grandma used chicken broth)
2 ½ cups water

Salt and pepper to taste

Minced fresh parsley

Wash and rinse the beans really well. Put everything except the parsley into a large pot and bring it to a boil.

Lower heat and let simmer for two hours. (Great-Grandma's recipe said to take out the bone around now, pull off the meat and mince it up, add it back in.)

Add some more broth and let it simmer while you make cornbread to go with it.

It takes about 3 hours to cook in total; the beans need to be tender.

Alternatively, put everything in a slow cooker and cook until beans are tender.

Serve with cornbread. Sprinkle parsley on top if desired.

GGM's Poor Man's Soup

1 quart jar of canned tomatoes – this would be 2 regular cans of tomatoes

1 quart of canned corn

1 finely chopped onion

1 clove of garlic

1 tsp dried celery leaves

Dried bread, cubed up. Amount varies depending on how much old bread you have.
Salt and pepper to taste

Dollop of butter

Put the tomatoes in the pot, bring to a boil, turn down to a simmer.

Add the onion, garlic, salt/pepper, and celery and simmer ten minutes.

Add the corn and simmer another few minutes.

Then toss in bread that is not moldy but has gotten hard from being several days old. The bread will absorb liquid and swell up.
Serve with a pat of butter on top of each bowl. It's good on a cold day and cheap.

GGM's Potato Soup

6 potatoes, peeled and cubed

Enough water to cover

1 onion, diced fine

2 tsp salt

1/2 tsp pepper

1 T chicken like or 1 cube bouillon

1 T butter or olive oil

1/2 cup white flour

Peel six potatoes or if they are new potatoes, just wash well and dice them.

Put potatoes in a pot, cover with water and cook til tender.

While they are cooking, add the onion, salt, pepper, bouillon, and butter.

While that cooks, get a good dry iron skillet. Put it over a low fire so it heats.

Add to it the fine white flour. Heat and constantly turn flour until it browns.

Add the browned flour to the cooked potatoes, stir until thickened.

Mom's White Chili

And back to recipes from other family members; this is one my mother altered to be vegetarian.

2 cups of chicken flavored TVP, reconstituted (TVP is Textured Vegetable Protein)

1 yellow onion diced

2 cloves garlic minced or smashed

24 ounces of vegetable broth

4 cans of great Northern beans drained and rinsed OR a pound of white northern beans that you have prepared beforehand by cooking as described earlier in this chapter. This is a good recipe for using the rest of a large pan of beans.

2 – 4 oz cans diced green chilies (She uses one hot, one mild)

1 can whole kernel corn, drained

1 tsp salt

1/2 tsp black pepper

1 tsp cumin

3/4 tsp oregano

1/2 tsp chili powder

1/4 tsp cayenne pepper

Small handful fresh cilantro, chopped

4 oz reduced fat cream cheese softened

1/4 cup half and half

TOPPINGS:

Sliced jalapenos

Sliced avocados

Dollop of sour cream

Minced fresh cilantro

Tortilla strips

Sliced olives

Shredded Monterey Jack or Mexican cheese

Put all of the ingredients except the cream cheese, half and half and cilantro in a pot and bring it to a boil.

Lower heat and simmer it for 45 minutes.

Blend together the cheese, half and half, and cilantro. Then add to the pot, stirring gently.

Let it simmer about 20 minutes more, then serve hot with any of the toppings listed, or whatever you please.

Cheeseburger Soup

This recipe was given to me by a friend when she heard I was writing up a recipe book. I altered it to be vegetarian – using vegetable protein instead of the ground beef. You can do this with a lot of recipes. It is delicious.

1 bag vegetarian beef-like crumbles, or 2 cups rehydrated beef-like TVP. (You can used cooked lentils or beans for protein, but it won't taste as cheeseburger-y.)

1 cup shredded carrots

1 cup chopped celery

1 cup chopped onions

2 T butter

6 cups vegetable broth or chicken-like broth

3 cups cubed potatoes

3 T butter

1/4 cup flour

3 cups milk

3 cups shredded cheddar cheese

In large pan, sauté the carrots, celery, and onions in 2 T butter until slightly softened.

Add vegetable protein, broth, and potatoes. Simmer until potatoes are soft

While that cooks, in another pan, combine 3 T butter and 1/4 cup flour to make a roux, stirring until browned. Slowly stir in the milk, stirring constantly to ensure smoothness. Mix in the cheese. Stir and heat until cheese is melted and it has thickened..

Check the potatoes in the other pan – once they're soft, add the cheese sauce to the main pot, mixing until it is all mixed together well.

Red Bean Chili

Chili is another recipe that has many, many variations. Here's the one I use most often, with the variations I use, depending on what's in my cupboards. Spices are the most variable; I change them up a bit almost every time I make it. This is a good baseline from which to experiment.

6 cups cooked kidney beans (you can use canned, or cook your own as is described earlier in the chapter. I usually cook my own.)

1 can corn, or 2 cups frozen or fresh corn

2 chopped bell peppers (It can make the chili look nice to have several colors of peppers, but green is usually cheapest.)

2 cans tomatoes, chopped, crushed, or blenderized (As you prefer; I know some people who hate chunky tomato in their food.)

1-2 cups other vegetables, chopped (celery, carrots, zucchini, summer squash are all good)
1 can tomato paste

1 chopped onion

3 chopped garlic cloves
2 T oil

2 bay leaves

1 tsp cumin

1 T dried oregano, or 2 T fresh

1-3 T chili powder (more is spicier)

1/4 -2 tsp chili flakes (more is spicier)

1/4 cup fresh chopped cilantro OR 1 ¼ T dried, optional (it's great if you like cilantro, not great if you're one of those who detests it)
1 bag vegetarian beef-like crumbles, *optional* (about 1 ½-2 cups)

Toppings (shredded cheese, sour cream, olives, lettuce, chopped jalapenos)

In large pan, sauté onion and garlic in the oil until golden brown.

Add the peppers, corn, and any other vegetables you're using and sauté until hot.

Add the tomatoes and spices and simmer for a few minutes.

Add the beans. Put on a lid and simmer for 45 minutes to an hour, until flavors are all blended and it's warm. Remember to remove the bay leaves after cooking.

If the beans are in a pot you've used to cook them, sauté the onions and vegetables as directed in a regular sized pan and add them to the beans. Then add the tomatoes and spices, cover, and simmer.

Alternative: To prepare in a slow cooker, sauté the onions and garlic in a frying pan. Put all ingredients in the slow cooker and mix together thoroughly. Cover and cook for 3-4 hours.

You can add a can or two of chopped green chili peppers, or fresh chopped jalapenos – it depends how much spice you like. Experiment with spices; I've seen recipes with much more, and recipes with less or with different ones.

Bean Chowder

1 pound white beans (great northern, navy beans, lima – can be all one kind, or a mix of beans)

1 ½ tsp salt (yes, different salt than the salt below)

1 cup chopped onion

1 ½ cup chopped celery

1/8 tsp black pepper

3 cups milk

1 can chopped tomatoes

1 can whole corn (or 2 cups frozen)

1/4 cup butter (half a stick)

1/4 cup flour

1/2 tsp salt

1 cup shredded Monterey Jack or cheddar cheese

Rinse, clean, and soak beans. In large kettle, boil them in 6-8 cups water until tender (If you're mixing beans, the lima beans don't need to boil as long, so add them when other beans are half done – about 2 1/2 hours for navy and great northern, and 1 hour for limas). Don't drain them.

While the beans are cooking, sauté onion and celery in a saucepan until onion is translucent.

Add the flour and mix well into a roux. Add salt and pepper.

Gradually mix in the milk, whisking all the while, and bring to a boil.

Remove from heat and add thickened milk to the beans. Stir until it's well mixed.

Add the remaining ingredients. Bring to a boil, and it's done.

You can make it spicier by adding some hot sauce or chilies, if you want.

Roasted Garlic Barley Soup

This recipe is time consuming, but is inexpensive, healthy, and good-tasting.

1 medium head garlic (yes, the whole head)

1 tsp oil

4 cups vegetable broth

1 ½ cups thinly sliced leeks. If you don't have leeks, use sliced green onions, or just chopped onion

3/4 cup thinly sliced celery

1 ½ tsp dried basil

1/8 tsp black pepper

1 can chopped tomatoes – do not drain

1 medium zucchini or summer squash, cut in half lengthwise and then sliced thin.

1/2 cup barley

Roast the garlic. To do this, peel away outer dry leaves without breaking up the head. Cut off about 1/4 inch of the top of the head, leaving the bulb intact but exposing individual cloves. Put entire head, cut side up, in a baking dish that has a lid and drizzle the oil over it. Bake at 400, covered, for 25 to 35 minutes, or until cloves feel soft when pressed. Cool slightly.

Press the garlic pulp from the individual cloves and mash the pulp with a fork.

If you are using quick-cooking barley, skip this step. If not, rinse barley and boil in water until tender, 45 minutes to an hour. Drain.

In a large pan, combine the garlic pulp, the vegetable broth, the leeks, celery, basil, and black pepper. Bring to a boil and reduce the heat.

Simmer, covered, for 10 minutes or until the celery and leeks are tender.

Add the tomatoes and their juice, the zucchini, and the barley. Return to boiling, then reduce heat and simmer, covered, for about 10 minutes.

Non-meats

The meat substitutes in most grocery stores are not cheap. That's not to say don't get them – you can plan them into your budget, and several of the recipes in this book use some. But they do tend to cost more than many other ingredients, and they are highly processed.

They are not your only choice. You can make some pretty darn tasty (and cheap) meat substitutes at home in your own kitchen.

These recipes are of things which would normally be meat, and now are not: recipes for your own sandwich patties, cottage cheese loaf (which is kind of like vegetarian meatloaf), and seitan.

Lentil Carrot Veggie Burgers

1/4 C finely chopped onion

1/4 C grated carrots

1/4 C water

3 cups cooked lentils, mashed

2 T fresh parsley, chopped (or 2 tsp dried parsley)

3 T tomato paste

3/4 C dried bread crumbs

salt to taste

oil for frying

Cook the onion and carrot in the water until tender, about ten minutes.

Drain off excess water, then combine the onion and carrot with the remaining ingredients and mix well.

Form into patties and fry in a lightly oiled frying pan until browned on both sides and heated through, about ten minutes (5 on each side). You can also form into patties, brush lightly with oil, and bake in the oven at 375, turning over halfway through.

Lentil-Potato Burgers

1/2 C chopped onion

3 celery stalks, chopped small

2 T olive oil

2 C cooked, drained and mashed up lentils

2 C mashed potatoes

1 C whole wheat or white bread crumbs, dried

1 tsp dried parsley or basil

1 ½ tsp dried sage

1 tsp ground thyme

salt & black pepper to taste

dried crushed pepper flakes to taste

Preheat oven to 350F

sauté onion and celery in oil until tender, then combine everything in a bowl and mix well.

Form patties and place on a well greased baking sheet. Bake about 15 minutes, then turn and bake another 15 minutes. You can fry these up in an oiled skillet too.

Cottage Cheese Loaf

There are hundreds of variations on this recipe; this is the one I use the most often. I'll put some ideas for switching it up underneath. It's basically a no-meat loaf, using cottage cheese, (and nuts if you can find them affordably), as the proteins.

2 T butter

1 small to medium onion, finely chopped
1-2 cloves garlic, finely chopped

2 T vegetarian bullion

3 eggs, beaten

1 tub cottage cheese

2-3 cups corn or wheat flakes, crushed

1 cup chopped walnuts or pecans (optional)

Preheat oven to 350

Grease a baking pan. The size can vary from loaf sized up to 8×11; larger pans will be thinner, the loaf pan will be more meatloaf like and will need to bake longer. I usually use a larger pan; I think it turns out better.

Melt the butter and sauté the onion and garlic until softened.

Mix everything together in a bowl until thoroughly blended.

Spoon into the pan and spread out evenly. Bake for 1 to 1 ½ hours.

This is another recipe where every cook has their own variation. A lot of people sauté a couple chopped celery stalks with the onions. Some add a tablespoon of soy sauce. There's a lot of variation on seasoning; my husband loves it when I add sage. A lot leave out the nuts, which are one of the most expensive ingredients. If I have nuts, I'll add them because I think it adds a nice texture. Some people skip all the seasonings and just add an envelope of dry onion soup mix. Some shred up a cup of carrots and add those. This is one of my husband's favorite foods; he'd happily eat it every week if I made it that often.

This recipe is great with mashed potatoes and gravy. Use the brown gravy recipe from the gravy and sauce chapter.

You can also form balls between the size of a walnut and a golf ball. Put these on a greased cookie sheet an inch or so apart and bake them for half an hour, until they are firm and dry on the outside. Meatballs! Serve with sauce, put on sandwiches, or add to spaghetti. You might want to add a little basil or oregano to them, if you're having them with pasta.

Oatmeal Patties

A woman at the church we attended when we lived in Michigan would bring them to potlucks; my husband got the recipe from her. He loves these things; when I was talking about putting together this book, this was one of a few recipes he asked me to include.

The Patties

3 cups quick oats

1 can condensed mushroom soup

2 eggs

1/4 to 1/2 tsp ground sage

1/2 tsp salt

scant 1 tsp garlic powder

1 small onion, finely chopped

Oil for frying

Grease a baking dish. Preheat oven to 350.

Mix all ingredients together. You can adjust the seasonings to suit, if you prefer less garlic or more sage.

Form into patties – mixture will make around 10 patties

Fry until brown on both sides and arrange in baking dish.

The Gravy

Combine:
1 can condensed mushroom soup

1/2 can water

Put mushroom soup into a bowl. Fill can halfway with water and pour into bowl (you can use the water to catch all the bits of soup that didn't come out).

Mix thoroughly; it will have a gravy-like consistency.

Pour over the patties in the baking dish.

Bake at 350 for 1 hour, so that onions are cooked and patties are cooked thoroughly.

Seitan

This is a basic wheat protein that you can make, and depending on how you season it, substitute for meat in a lot of ways. There are a couple ways to make it. The shortest is to use already-separated vital wheat gluten flour; it's also more costly, since a couple cups of vital wheat gluten costs more than an entire bag of whole wheat flour. The other way is, as you could guess, uses whole wheat flour. Either way costs less than most of the pre-made meat substitutes out there. It takes a little practice, but you end up with completely malleable meat substitute that is whatever flavor you desire.

To make seitan, first you make the dough, then you simmer it slowly in a broth. During the simmering, it soaks of up the flavor of the broth and more than doubles in size. You can completely alter the flavor of the seitan by how you season the broth.

Seitan made from Whole Wheat Flour

4 cups whole wheat flour

1 quart water

Lots of rinsing water. Lots.

Put the flour in a mixing bowl and add enough water to make a soft, kneadable dough – about 1 2/3 cups. Knead the dough for about 5 minutes, then add enough water to cover the dough and set aside for 15 minutes.

While it's resting, make your broth. A very basic broth is half a sliced onion. a clove of chopped garlic, and 2 T of soy sauce in 1 quart of water. Bring the broth to a boil, then lower to a simmer until the dough is ready. This is only a start – the broth will soak up whatever flavors you use, so consider making chicken flavor, beef flavor, and so on with different vegetarian broths and different seasoning blends.

Okay, back to the dough. Pop the bowl of dough and water in the sink and start kneading. You're going to be kneading a lot. Knead it until the water starts turning white and milky; that is the starch getting worked out. Dump out that water, rinse the dough, refill, and knead again. The water will get white. Repeat. Keep repeating knead-rinse-knead-rinse until the water stays mostly clear. <u>This will take multiple rinses.</u>

Now, put the dough in the broth; if you don't want one big lump, you can make smaller lumps or shapes. Do not allow the broth to boil. At all. It needs to slowly cook the dough; the slower it cooks, the more solid the texture of the finished seitan. Keep it at a low simmer for at least an hour.

Remove seitan from the broth and let cool. Do not discard the broth; you'll store the seitan in it. It will keep for 4 or 5 days, covered and in broth, in the fridge. Or you can freeze it – in broth – and keep for weeks.

Seitan made from Vital Wheat Gluten

1 cup vital wheat gluten

1/4 cup chickpea or soy flour

1 cup water

Sift together the gluten and chickpea or soy flour.

Add the water and knead for 5 minutes.

Set aside while you make your broth. Bring it to a boil, then lower it to a simmer.

Cut dough into several pieces, slices, or chunks, and put in the broth.

Simmer – do not boil – one hour, uncovered.

Remove from heat and set aside to cool. Once cooled, cut into whatever shapes you want.

Refrigerate in broth, covered, or freeze in broth.

Black Bean Burgers 2 Ways

These are hearty and cheap; good for budgets, and also good for you –
no super-processed anything, lots of fiber.

5 cups (or 3 cans) cooked black beans

1 1/2 cups rolled oats

1 medium onion, chopped fine or grated

2 jalapeno peppers, de-seeded and chopped

3/4 cup chopped fresh cilantro

2 large eggs, lightly beaten

1 tsp salt

1/4 cup flour

1/4 cup cornmeal

1 T oil

Mash the beans with a fork

Add the oats, onion, jalapenos, cilantro, eggs, and salt. Mix well. A
good way to mix is to just squish it all together with your hands. It
will be very wet; if it's too liquid to handle, let it soak for a while; the
oats will soak up some moisture. Or chill; that thickens it some.

Shape into patties – should make 8-10, depending how large you
make them.

Mix the flour and cornmeal together.

Roll the patties in the flour mixture, then cook them over medium
heat for 5 minutes each side, or until they are golden brown.

Serve on hamburger buns with condiments and toppings of your
choice.

Jalapenos and cilantro not your thing? You can leave them out entirely, which will be a little bland, but not bad.

Or try this other recipe, which I made for dinner just tonight.

5 cups (or 3 cans) cooked black beans

1 ½ cups rolled oats

1 medium onion, chopped fine or grated

1 finely chopped green pepper

2 pressed cloves garlic

1 tsp cumin

1 T chili powder

2 large eggs, lightly beaten

1 tsp salt

1/4 cup flour

1/4 cup cornmeal

1 T oil

Mash the beans with a fork

Add the oats, onion, pepper, spices, eggs, and salt. Mix well.

Shape into patties.

Mix the flour and cornmeal together.

Dredge the patties in the flour mixture, then cook them over medium heat for 5 minutes each side, or until they are golden brown.

Serve on hamburger buns with condiments and toppings of your choice.

If you want milder or softer onions and/or garlic, you can sauté them in a bit of oil before mixing them in with the beans.

If you don't have enough black beans, you can use other beans instead or to supplement the black beans.

Casseroles and Entrees

Casseroles are simply foods that are baked slowly in a casserole dish. This means the things that count as casseroles were limited only by the ingenuity of cooks over the ages. They might be side dishes, but are often one-dish meals – grains, dairy, vegetables, sauces, all baked together in a complete whole, needing only bread or a salad to round out the meal.

Some are elaborate – lasagna, for instance. Sometimes they are fast and easy.

They can be very nutritious, or not so much. They're a great way to use leftovers, or small bits of remaining ingredients after cooking other things. (that lone carrot and half onion, a leftover sprig of basil, some mashed potatoes – boom, casserole.)

I'm also including entrees, the main dishes that make the bulk of a meal. These often overlap the casserole or are a kind of casserole, but not always; I've got curries and stir-fries in this section too.

Mom's Zucchini Boats

This could be either a main dish or a side dish; I usually eat it as a main dish, and my husband as a side. Mom found it and altered it to suit her when she had to look for new recipes after she became diabetic – this is low-carb and diabetic-friendly.

3 small to medium zucchini

1 cup finely shredded mozzarella, 3 T set aside.
1 package of cream cheese (8 ounces), brought to room temperature
1 egg

2 cloves garlic, either chopped fine or pressed through garlic press

2 tsp Italian seasoning blend

Salt and pepper to taste (start with 1/2 tsp each)

1/4 cup chopped pecans or pine nuts

3 T Parmesan

Fill large pan with water and bring it to a boil. Wash zucchini and cut off the stem end. Boil zucchini for about 15 minutes to partially cook them, then pour out boiling water and fill pan with cold water to cool them off.

Preheat oven to 350 and grease a baking dish.

When cool, cut zucchini in half. Scoop out the seeds. Set zucchini, hollow side up, in the baking dish.

Mix together mozzarella, cream cheese, egg, garlic, Italian seasoning, salt, pepper, and most of the pecans.

Spoon cheese mixture into zucchini. Use spoon to make an indent in the top of each. Sprinkle in remaining mozzarella, nuts, and Parmesan.

Bake for about 35 minutes, until zucchini is nicely soft and cheese is melted and bubbly. If you want less browned zucchini and cheese, baked covered until last ten minutes, then uncover. Uncovered is browner and drier, covered is moister and less brown.

The original recipe called for pine nuts, which are rather expensive. You could skip nuts if they are too costly in your area or at this time of year.

Egg Noodle All-in-One Meal

I make this pretty frequently; it's another of my husband's favorites, and it's easy and cheap. This is an outline that's usable with whatever kind of veggies and cheese I have at hand. It's quick and easy and is a fairly complete meal.

2-3 cups egg noodles, dry – preferably whole grain (or use Grandma's recipe)

1/2-1 C shredded cheese

1 bag frozen vegetables

Optional – vegetarian meat substitute, sautéed firm tofu cubes, or seitan, cut into small pieces

2 T butter

Salt and Pepper to taste

Other seasonings as desired (I'll often add a pinch of dried garlic or onion powder, or a couple tsp of basil or tarragon, or some bouillon dissolved in some of the pasta water.)

Cook the egg noodles, drain, and return to pan or put in a large bowl.

While pasta is cooking, steam the veggies (or zap them in the microwave till hot). Add to bowl with pasta after it's drained.

Add butter and stir until it melts. Add pepper, salt, seasonings, and cheese and stir. Add non-meat.

Mix everything together. Serve.

This includes vegetables, whole grains, and protein. Good blends to start with include non-chicken, Colby-jack, spinach, and tarragon, or non-beef, cheddar, broccoli, onion, and oregano.

Slow Cooker Curried Rice and Lentils

I don't even remember where I got this one; it's on my ongoing recipe file. It's thicker than a soup, really, the rice and lentils both soak up the broth.

1 cup brown rice

1 tbsp curry powder

3 ½ cups broth

1/2 cup lentils

2 bouillon cubes (either vegetable bouillon, or non-chicken chickenish)

1/2 tsp garlic powder

1/4 tsp pepper

1 onion, diced

Combine all the ingredients in a slow cooker. Cover and cook on low for 4 to 5 hours. Makes four servings.

If you do not have a slow cooker, you can put the ingredients a regular pot, cover tightly, and cook on low-medium until the lentils and rice are soft and the fluid is mostly soaked up; stirring occasionally. Be careful not to burn it. It will only take about 20 minutes.

Mazidra – Lebanese Lentil and Onions

4 cups water

1 cup brown lentils, rinsed and picked over

1/2 tsp salt

1-2 tsp non-chicken seasoning/broth, like McKay's, or Washington's

3-4 cloves garlic – can be whole, sliced, diced, or pressed through a garlic press

1 bay leaf

1-3 large onions

2 T olive oil

Prepared Rice

In a large pan, combine water, lentils, seasoning, garlic, bay leaf, and salt. Bring to a boil, cover, and simmer for 30-40 minutes. Remove lid.

Make rice.

Slice onions and sauté in oil in a frying pan until soft and translucent.

To serve, put rice on plate. Ladle lentils over that, and top with soft onion rings.

Dahl

1 cup red lentils

2 cups water

1 T olive oil

1 tsp salt

1/2 tsp ground turmeric

1/4 tsp ground coriander

1/8 tsp cayenne

2/3 cup chopped onion

1 T olive oil

1 T minced garlic

1 ½ tsp fresh ginger, minced (can use 1/8 tsp dried, but there will be a difference in flavor)

2 T water

1 T tomato paste

1/2 T cumin seeds, whole and toasted

Rinse lentils well, and soak in warm water for 30 minutes, then drain.

In medium saucepan, combine lentils, 2 cups water, salt, turmeric, coriander, and cayenne.

Simmer for 30 minutes, until lentils are tender. Reduce heat and keep warm.

In frying pan, sauté onions in oil until golden brown and tender. Add garlic and ginger and sauté another 5 minutes.

Add 2 T water and tomato paste and mix well.

Add sauce to lentils and stir well

To toast cumin seeds – in small, dry frying pan, put seeds and heat over med-high heat until they start to smell good.

Stir into dahl. Serve with rice and bread. (Chapati or roti if you have it.)

Ginger Garlic Broccoli Stir Fry

I usually make this one by winging it – toss stuff in the skillet till it looks right. I made it again for this book, while writing down what I was doing. But you need to know it's a pretty flexible recipe, and you can fiddle till you get it the way you want.

1/2 onion, chopped

2 T oil

1 bag frozen chopped broccoli, thawed, or 3 cups chopped broccoli

1/2 -1 tsp garlic powder OR 1-2 garlic cloves, pressed or chopped

1 T soy sauce

1 T fresh ginger or 1/8-1/4 tsp ground ginger

1 to 2 tsp McKay's or other seasoning bouillon mix (optional)

1/2 to 1 cup tofu, seitan, vegetarian meat substitute (optional)

Sauté the onion in the oil until golden brown.

Add the broccoli and mix together. Add a couple tablespoons of water if necessary to keep it from sticking; you'll need to let the water simmer off before serving, so don't add too much if you add it.

Mix in soy sauce, ginger, and seasoning. (Seasoning mix is optional; whether I use it or not depends on the protein I've used. Tofu's bland, so needs seasoning. Some meat substitutes come in a broth, so then it's not needed.) Stir well.

Add the protein. Simmer all together until the broccoli is desired softness and any extra fluid has simmered off.

Serve over rice.

I always chop my onions fine, because my husband's picky about onions. You can have larger pieces or use those tiny whole onions if you prefer. You can add other vegetables; try with some green or red peppers, cauliflower (which needs more cooking time, so cook it first), or spinach.

I find that I rather prefer dried to fresh ginger in this, though both are good. Dried costs less, so that is something to keep in mind.

I'll often use more garlic than this, but I like garlic a lot. I kept it a bit light in this recipe, since I know not everyone likes garlic as much as I do. Feel free to add more if you, too, love garlic.

Cauliflower Curry

1 bag frozen cauliflower, chopped or 1 head cauliflower, chopped

1 can coconut milk

1-3 cloves garlic, pressed

1 chopped onion

2 T oil

3 tsp curry powder

OR

1/2 tsp cumin

1/2 tsp coriander

1/2 tsp turmeric

pinch red pepper

pinch dried ginger, or 1/2 tsp fresh minced ginger

1 cup vegetarian protein – tofu, seitan, artificial chicken, cooked legumes

Sauté onion in oil for a few minutes, add the garlic, sauté until golden brown.

Combine onion, cauliflower, and spices and simmer until cauliflower is mostly done.

Add in protein and cook until cauliflower is tender and protein is heated through.

Serve over rice.

You can add shredded carrots to this and it's delicious, or use half potatoes and half cauliflower.

Haystacks

I've been told this is called Texas Straw Hat in other places, but haystacks is what I've heard it called my entire life. It's great for potlucks or groups of people; you can assign each person to bring an ingredient or two in enough quantities for however large a group you have.

1 bag corn tortilla chips

1 batch chili, prepared according to your favorite recipe OR 1 pan cooked beans

2 cups shredded cheddar or Mexican cheese

1 head lettuce, washed and shredded

2 tomatoes, chopped

1 small onion, chopped (more if you have a lot of onion-loving people)

1 can black olives, sliced (when we have it, we usually use 2, because olives are delicious)
1 can green olives, sliced

1 container sour cream

Chopped jalapenos, if anyone likes them

Set everything out in bowls, with serving spoons. Each person at dinner makes their own, layering up chips, chili, cheese, lettuce, and whatever toppings they like. This is great with youth groups, kids parties, potlucks, or gatherings. For large groups, just get more of everything, or assign each person to bring x amount of one of the ingredients.

You can add other toppings, if you think of any you want. I've had them before with a bowl of corn, or of chopped carrots to use for toppings.

If you don't want everything laid out, you can mix it all together like a salad. The chips go soggy very fast, though, so I don't like that as much.

Pot Pie

This is a great one for using whatever vegetables you've got; you can substitute in for the ones listed here if you need to use up leftovers.

1 double crust pie crust, as directed in pie chapter

1/2 onion, chopped

2 T oil

2 chopped carrots

1-2 chopped celery

1 ½ T flour

3/4 cup water

2 tsp vegetable bouillon

1/2 cup peas

1/2 cup green beans

1/2 cup corn

2 potatoes, peeled if needed and cut into 1/2-3/4 inch cubes

2 tsp dried parsley

1/2 tsp dried thyme

1/2 tsp pepper

Boil the potatoes in water until almost tender, drain and set aside. You can also steam the carrots to ensure they are tender if desired. I don't usually; they cook up fine during baking.

Sauté the onion in the oil in a large pan until translucent, mix in the flour to make a roux.

Gradually add the water and bouillon, mixing the entire time to assure smoothness of the gravy.

Add the herbs and vegetables. Mix everything together and simmer for 5 minutes or so, then remove from heat.

Roll out the bottom crust, if you're using a bottom crust (some people prefer to only use a top crust in their pot pies, and that is also tasty), and press into your pie plate.

Put filling in the pie.

Roll out and place the top crust, crimping well around edges and cutting ventilation slices in top (or use a pie bird).

Bake for 35 minutes or so, until crust is golden brown. Let stand a few minutes before cutting.

Other Options:

Now, this recipe is a starting point. There's a lot you can do with a pot pie. To begin with, you can put any kind of stew inside.

You can have a top and bottom crust, or just a top crust. If you need more, make more filling and bake it in a 9×13 inch pan instead of a pie plate.

You don't have to use a pie crust. Try putting the filling in a 9×13 baking pan, then topping with a batch of biscuits (homemade or canned).

Use other veggies – cauliflower is good. A nice cauliflower potato curry, like the one in this book, makes an interesting potpie; serve it with a scoop of cottage cheese.

Add vegetarian meat substitutes for chicken-like or beef-like potpies. Or sprinkle non-bacon bits over it when you serve it.

The lentil filling from the shepherd's pie recipe is good in a potpie too.

Try adding a can of cream of mushroom or cream of celery soup instead of the gravy/roux mix – add whatever vegetables you have to the can of soup and half a can of water or milk. Mix them all together and use as the pie filling.

Colcannon Bake

This is a traditional Irish recipe. There are a TON of variations on it, with different proportions of potatoes and cabbage, different seasonings, and different add-ins. Consider experimenting with it till you find your favorite. I'll put some suggestions underneath the recipe.

2 C Mashed potatoes

3 C shredded cabbage

1 chopped onion

1 C shredded cheddar

1 egg

1/2 cup whole milk, half and half, or heavy cream.
3 T olive oil

Preheat oven to 350.

Sauté the onion for a few minutes, then add the cabbage and sauté it all together, stirring occasionally, until the pieces get translucent and start to be softer. Add 1/4 to 1/2 cup water for the sautéing, so that it doesn't stick. The water will steam off most of the way while it cooks. Don't use too much; the point is for a little steam and less sticking, not for liquid.

In a large bowl, mix together mashed potatoes, egg, and milk.

Add the cabbage/onion mix and 3/4 of the cheese.

Bake in covered casserole dish for 40 to 60 minutes. Put remaining cheese on top; add more if you want. Bake with lid off until cheese is melted and bubbly.

This is a great recipe for using leftovers mashed potatoes or leftover cabbage. You can toss in other things as well, if you want, but they might not match. A lot of traditional recipes include ham, bacon, or some other form of pork; I obviously don't use that, I will sometimes use vegetarian sandwich slices or a veggie bacon chopped up and mixed in before the mixture is put in the dish to bake.

I'll often add chopped garlic. Green onions and/or chives can be a tasty addition too. I've seen some recipes that use leeks, but I've never tried that.

If you want vegan, skip the dairy and egg. The purpose of the egg is to help it stick together; it will be less solid without it, but otherwise be fine. Add some water and a couple tablespoons of oil to get the mixture soft, if that's needed.

You can use 1/2 cup sour cream instead of the milk or cream; you can use more or less of both to get the consistency you want.

Tater Tot Casserole

There are a bazillion recipes for this hot dish. This is the one I use.

1 regular bag frozen tater tots

1 can cream of mushroom or cream of celery

2 cans green beans, drained
3/4 cup milk

1/2 tsp garlic powder

1 tsp onion powder, or ½ onion chopped fine

2 cups shredded cheddar

1 package vegetarian hamburgers, optional

Preheat oven to 350 and grease a large baking dish.

In large bowl, mix soup and milk.

Add seasonings, green beans, and half the cheese.

Mix in the tater tots. Depending on the kind of hamburger substitute you get and personal preferences, you can either crumble it and mix it in at this point, or save for next step.;

Spread mixture in baking dish. If you want, you can put hamburger substitute on top of casserole here instead of mixing in with the rest of the ingredients.

Top with remaining cheese and bake for 45-60 minutes, or until cheese is melted and mixture is hot all the way through and bubbly.

You can layer everything and pour the soup over it before covering with cheese, if you prefer; if you do that, usually the tater tots are carefully laid on top to make a kind of crust.

You can use other vegetables instead of only green beans; try with a bag of frozen mixed veggies, or with peas or corn instead of, or along with, the green beans.

Summer Squash Casserole

This is good in the summer when zucchini and yellow squash are either taking over your garden, or available cheap at farmer's markets and groceries.

1 small onion, chopped fine

2 cloves garlic, chopped or pressed

1 T butter

4 cups summer squashes, sliced fine or cubed. (I like to slice mine on a mandolin; some people prefer chunks.)

1 tsp salt

1/2 tsp pepper

1 cup shredded cheese (cheddar, Colby, and Monterey Jack work well)

1/3 cup bread crumbs or crushed crackers.

1/2 cup heavy cream

2 eggs

Preheat oven to 400 and grease a 9×13 inch baking dish.

Sauté onion and garlic in the butter in a frying pan until translucent.

Add the squash, salt, and pepper and sauté about 5 minutes, until soft. (less for thinner squash, more for thicker cubes). Transfer to mixing bowl.

Mix in half the cheese and the crumbs.

Beat the eggs and cream together, and mix into the squash mixture.

Pour into baking dish and top with the rest of the cheese.

Bake about half an hour, until golden brown and bubbling.

You can add other seasonings, especially if you've got fresh herbs in the summer. Try tarragon or rosemary.

Cheesy Potato Casserole

6-8 potatoes, peeled and sliced. Should be about 6 or so cups of potatoes.

2 cups white sauce, prepared as described in sauce chapter

1/2 small onion, sliced thin or chopped fine

Pepper to taste; I like a couple teaspoons

1 cup strongly flavored shredded cheese – sharp cheddar is good

Heat oven to 400. Grease a 9×13 or 1 ½ quart baking dish.

Mix the onion with the white sauce and the pepper. Put a little white sauce in the pan bottom, then a layer of potatoes, then more sauce, then cheese, and continue layering until all potatoes, sauce, and cheese are used up. Be sure top layer is cheese.

Bake for 30 minutes, until potatoes are tender and cheese is bubbly and browned a bit. You can bake covered for the first twenty minutes or so if you want a moister casserole

Sometimes I've seen this made with mushroom soup or cream of celery instead of white sauce; I like the white sauce better, but see what you prefer.

For a shorter baking time, you can partially bake the potatoes in the microwave and let them cool before removing peel and slicing. You won't be able to slice as thin, and they may be a little crumbly. That's not necessarily a bad thing; different kinds of potatoes will have different textures as well. Some are more dense and moist, and some more dry and crumbly naturally.

Not-Shepherd's Pie

Shepherd's pie got the name because it included lamb, so this no-meat recipe isn't quite that. Nowadays, the name for the dish has evolved to refer to a thick, stew-like filling topped with mashed potatoes. It is warm, tasty, and hearty. This recipe is a little more of a formula at points; you can change up the seasonings, or skip the lentils (cutting the broth down to one or two cups) and focus on the vegetables. (If you do that, you'll need a lot more vegetables to have enough stew.)

8 or 9 potatoes, peeled and cut into 1 inch cubes

Water for boiling them

4 T butter

Salt and pepper to taste
Milk enough to thin if needed

1/2 cup shredded cheese (Optional)

1 onion, chopped

2-3 cloves garlic, chopped or pressed

2 T oil
1 ½ cup lentils, rinsed and picked over

4 cups broth – vegetable broth, or non-meat beeflike broth (McKay's, Washington's, or the like)

2 cups vegetables. (You can just use a bag of frozen mixed, or make your own vegetable blend based on what you've got. Carrots, corn, parsnips, peas, green beans, celery, and cabbage are all good for this. You can also add 2-3 T tomato paste, if you want a tomato flavor.)
Seasonings – to taste. Try 2 tsp dried rosemary and a couple bay leaves (remember to remove the bay leaves after cooking, or use ground), or 1 tsp thyme, and/or 1 tsp sage.

Heat oven to 400 and grease a 9×13 inch baking dish, or a 2 quart casserole dish. (You can do this after you've started cooking the potatoes and lentils, if you don't want to keep the oven going the whole cooking time.)

Cook the potatoes in the water until they are soft, then mash them with the butter. Add a little milk, 1 T at a time, if you need to make the potatoes a bit wetter. Mix in the cheese with the potatoes, if you are using it.

In a large cooking pot, sauté the onions and garlic until they are softened and lightly browned.

Add the broth, lentils, and seasonings to the pot. Bring to a boil, then lower heat to a simmer and cook 35 minutes or so, until lentils are tender.

Add the vegetables after 25 minutes. If you're using a dense vegetable, like carrots or parsnips, add them a little earlier so they get a bit more cooking time. Stir and cover.

If you want a thicker sauce, you can make a roux and mix it in, or mix some cornstarch and water or broth (about 2 T of cornstarch in enough water to have a runny mix) and mix in with the stew.

Taste and adjust seasonings if needed. Spoon stew into baking dish.

Top carefully with mashed potatoes. If you just dump the potatoes on, they won't spread over the top; you'll get a lump of mashed potatoes in the middle of a sea of stew. You can drop it by spoonfuls across the top, then spread gently. You can also put it in a Ziploc bag, seal it up, then cut off one corner and squeeze it out. You can also use a frosting dispenser, as in cake decorating, and make designs. I tend towards 'simpler is better', and use a spoon. but you have options.

Place baking dish on a cookie sheet, to catch any fluid that might boil out while it bakes, and put in the oven.

Bake for 15 minutes, or until potatoes turn golden-brown.

Breads

Bread is a staple food in most areas of the world. It comes in many shapes, forms, and recipes, but anywhere there is grain, there are varieties of bread.

Bread can be made from grains (wheat, rice, corn, barley, oats), legumes, potatoes, and nuts. It can be not raised at all, or raised with baking powder, yeast, or sourdough.

Bread can be sweet (zucchini bread, blueberry muffins) or savory (cheese bread, pizza). It can have spices, toppings, additions, or be very plain. It's been used as a plate and means of preservation – trenchers (used in medieval times as plates, then eaten themselves) and pies (originally a way to store and carry food; sometimes the crust wasn't even eaten), and as a delicious food all on its own.

Quickbreads are called that because they are comparatively fast to prepare. You don't have to wait over an hour for the first raise, then another 3/4 of an hour for the second raise, and only then bake your bread. You just mix them up and pop them in the oven. There are a lot of types of quickbreads, ranging from biscuits to banana bread. I'll include a wide sampling, along with ways to personalize them.

You can also make muffins out of most quick breads. Simply line muffin tins with paper liners (or oil and flour them, or use a thorough application of cooking spray), fill each cup 75-80% full, and bake for about 1/2 to 2/3s of the time a loaf would take. Keep an eye on them; they are done when a skewer or toothpick stuck in the middle of a muffin comes out clean.

Basic Bread Recipe

This recipe is a very basic bread; I learned how to make this as soon as I was old enough to reach the tabletop. You can do all kinds of thing to alter it; I'll put some suggestions at the end. You can use it for bread, dinner rolls, pizza crust, rather chewy cinnamon rolls (think closer to cinnamon bread) - all kinds of dough-based goodness.

2 ¼ cup warm water

2 tsp yeast (or 1 envelope)

1/4 cup sugar

1 ½ tsp salt

3 T oil

6 to 6 ¾ cup flour

Put the yeast in a cup of water with a spoon of sugar. Stir, and let sit for 5 minutes, until the yeast gets bubbly.

Put to the rest of your water in a large mixing bowl. Add the rest of the sugar, the oil, and salt, and stir together. Add the flour, a cup at a time, stirring thoroughly. When you can't stir with a spoon, start to knead the flour in. It should be firm, but still a little sticky. That should go away while you knead it. Turn onto a floured board or counter. (If you use the counter, be sure to wash it REALLY well first.) Knead for 5-10 minutes; this helps activate the gluten and gives the bread a nice texture.

Cover with a clean cloth and let sit in a warm spot until it doubles in size. Punch down and knead.

Divide into loaves, rolls, or other. Remember it will grow; your pieces should be about half the size you actually want the finished product to be. Shape and put into greased baking dish.

Allow to raise for about half an hour. While bread is raising the second time, preheat oven to 350.

Bake for 35 minutes or so, until it is golden brown on top and makes a 'thunk' noise when you tap it with a fingernail.

Remove from oven. I butter the top while it's hot; this softens it. If you prefer a crisper crust, just allow to cool. Keep stored in an airtight bag or container to prevent it from drying out.

Options for switching it up:

You can use honey instead of sugar, but use about a third less honey, as it's sweeter. Reduce the water as well, by slightly less than the amount of honey you used. Same for using maple syrup instead of sugar. These are more costly than sugar, unless you make your own syrup or have bees. They make a moister bread, and add a delicious flavor to bread.

You can add milk as a substitute for some or all of the water. You can also add powdered milk, which might be cheaper.

The oil is technically optional; I think it improves the texture, but you can try without it and see what you think.

This recipe uses white flour, for ease as you're learning. Switch part or all of that out for whole grain flour. If you do that, you may need slightly less flour; whole grain flour seems, to me, to soak up a bit more of the water. I never use only white flour; I usually go about half and half, or even three-quarters wheat. You can change out some or all of of the flour for whole grain flour.

You can add in oatmeal, or wheat germ, or other ground grains. Remember to use less flour accordingly; oats soak up water. Honey-oatmeal dinner rolls are delicious. You'll get a feel for how finished dough should feel, and that will make it easier when subbing in different kinds of flours and grains.

You can flatten out a piece of dough for a pizza crust; this doesn't necessarily need a second raising, but can be put directly into a 450 degree oven. (If you want a thicker, bread-ier crust, go ahead and let it raise.) Or you can roll it out thin, put toppings on only one half, fold the other half over, seal WELL all around the edges (try rolling them a bit, and pinching together), brush olive oil or garlic butter over the top, and make stromboli. If all you want is pizza crust, reduce the sugar for a less sweet crust and consider not adding the oil at all.

You can roll out the dough thin, and cover with cinnamon sugar and dabs of butter. Roll it up again, being sure to seal all the edges, and curl it into a baking dish. Let raise, and bake as for bread. This makes a very firm cross between cinnamon roll and cinnamon bread.

You can roll out a loaf of bread's worth of dough to a longish rectangle the width of your loaf pan and 1/2-3/4 of an inch thick, then roll all kinds of stuff up in it for different breads. Try butter and herbs, cheese, cranberries and nuts, chocolate and marshmallows (or caramel), or Nutella.

For dinner rolls, cut off pieces of dough about the size of an egg and shape by pinching what will be the bottom until round. Put in baking dish and allow to raise, then bake for 25ish minutes. You can put things into the middle and form the roll around the filling; cheese is delicious for this.

Mom's Banana Bread

When I got my first apartment, I emailed my Mom asking how to make banana bread. Here's the recipe she sent me (edited a bit for clarity; she was having a bad day).

5-6 ripe (or over ripe) bananas

2 cups flour

2 eggs

1/2 cup brown sugar

1/4 cup white sugar

1 tsp baking soda

1 ½ tsp baking powder

1 tsp vanilla or walnut flavoring

Mash bananas up with a fork. Combine everything together and put into loaf pans. Bake at 350 for one hour, until skewer or knife pushed into center comes out moist and mostly clean (only a few crumbs, not batter).

This recipe is a little unusual in that it has less sugar and no added oil. It makes a very moist bread due to all the fruit, so keep refrigerated or eat all up in a day or two, before it grows mold. I find it tastes better the next day, after a night spent wrapped in parchment paper for some of the extra moisture to dry a bit. It's got a much chewier texture than the second kind of banana bread, and, between the lower added sugar, tripled amount of fruit, and no added oil, is healthier. It's very good with peanut butter and a handful of dried cranberries spread over it.

Regular Banana Bread

1 ¾ cups flour

2 tsp baking powder

1/2 tsp salt

2/3 cup sugar

1/3 cup oil or butter
2 eggs
2 ripe bananas, mashed

1 tsp vanilla (optional)

Preheat oven to 350 and grease a bread pan.

Mix the flour, baking powder, and salt together in one bowl.

Mix the eggs, oil, bananas, and sugar together in another mixing bowl. You can do this by hand (I usually do), but for the greatest smoothness, run them through a blender.

Add the dry ingredients and mix just until combined.

Pour into greased pan and bake for about 45 minutes, until lightly browned and a skewer inserted in center comes out mostly clean, with just a few crumbs and no batter. Turn out onto a cooling rack or a clean towel. It will cool faster on the rack, but even just on a towel will be faster than staying in the hot pan.

Ideas for variation: You can add half a cup of chopped nuts, or chocolate chips, or peanut butter chips, or chopped dried fruit. You can try different spices as well; a quarter tsp of cinnamon, or some nutmeg. There are a lot of variations on banana bread.

Ginger Zucchini Bread

Zucchini are some of the most ubiquitous and cheapest vegetables of the summer. They are very easy to grow, and you can shred zucchini, squeeze out the extra water, and freeze for use year round. There are a TON of recipes using it; zucchini bread is some of the most popular, and no wonder. It's absolutely delicious. There are many variations on zucchini bread – I'll include a few. This recipe was given to me by a woman at church; I have it in a recipe scrapbook, written on a 3 by 5 card. It makes one loaf.

1 ½ cups flour

1 tsp ginger

1/4 tsp cinnamon (optional; if used, it might be more prominent than the ginger)

1 ½ tsp baking powder

1/4 tsp salt

1 cup granulated sugar

1/4 cup oil

2 eggs

Grated peel and juice from ½ lemon or lime (or 1/2 tsp dried lemon/lime peel and 1 T of lemon/lime juice)

1 cup shredded zucchini, squeezed lightly to get out extra moisture. (Don't over-squeeze; there are other recipes where you squeeze the dickens out of the zucchini, this isn't one.)

Preheat oven to 350 and grease a loaf pan and dust it with flour (or spray it with cooking spray).

Combine flour, ginger, cinnamon (if you're using it) baking powder, salt, and sugar. Mix well.

Add oil, eggs, lemon/lime peel and juice, and zucchini. Stir together – don't over stir, just until moistened and no lumps.

Pour into loaf pan and smooth top.

Bake 50-60 minutes, or until toothpick or skewer inserted into center of bread comes out clean.

Let rest 5-10 minutes, then turn out onto wire rack and cool completely.

If you don't have a wire rack, turn carefully onto a clean tea towel. Turn right side up and let cool completely.

You can change out the seasonings, if you want. A lot of zucchini breads don't include ginger, but 1-2 tsp cinnamon and 1/4-1/2 tsp nutmeg.
You can add 1/2-3/4 cups chocolate chips, raisins, or chopped nuts, if desired.

Lemon-Blueberry Zucchini Bread

Around here, blueberries and zucchini are in season at the same time, so the berries are less than they are at other times. You can use frozen berries, if that's more affordable. Or skip them entirely; it's still delicious.

2 eggs lightly beaten, room temperature

1/2 cup vegetable oil

1 ½ tsp vanilla extract

3/4 cup white sugar

1 cup shredded and lightly squeezed zucchini (should be damp, not dripping wet or over dry)

3/4 tsp dried lemon peel or zest of half a lemon

Juice of half a lemon, or 1 T lemon juice

1 ½ cups flour

1/2 tsp salt

1/2 tsp baking powder

scant 1/4 tsp baking soda

1 cup fresh blueberries

Preheat oven to 350. Grease a loaf pan.

In one bowl, mix together dry ingredients (flour, salt, baking powder, baking soda) and set aside.

In large bowl, beat together eggs, oil, vanilla, sugar, lemon juice, and lemon zest.

Fold in zucchini with rubber spatula.

Mix in dry ingredients, a third at a time.

Fold in blueberries gently.

Scrape batter into loaf pan and bake for 45 minutes, or until skewer stuck into center comes out moist and mostly clean.

Another option for this recipe is to double it and bake it in cake pans (lined with parchment paper). Turn them out to cool, and once they are cool, make a batch of cream cheese frosting. Add a little lemon juice and lemon zest or dried peel to the frosting, if you want. Put it all together to make a delicious lemon-blueberry layer cake and garnish with more blueberries.

You can use raspberries or dried cranberries, instead of blueberries, if you want. Or skip berries and put in 1-2 T poppyseeds.

Chocolate Chocolate Chip Zucchini Bread

This is a dessert bread, with a good portion of vegetables in it. It tastes like a chocolate pound cake, almost, but contains squash along with the chocolate chips.

1 cup flour

1/2 cup cocoa

1 tsp baking soda

1/2 tsp salt

2 eggs

1 tsp vanilla (alternatively, 1 T strong espresso or 1 tsp instant coffee)
1/2 cup oil or melted butter, cooled down, or combination of both

3/4 cup brown sugar, packed

1 ½ cups shredded zucchini, packed

1 cup chocolate chips, with 1/4 cup held separately to be sprinkled on top instead of mixed in.

Preheat oven to 350 and grease a loaf pan.

Sift together flour, cocoa, baking soda, and salt in one bowl.

In large bowl, mix egg, vanilla (or coffee), oil, and sugar. Beat until smooth.

Mix the dry ingredients into the egg mixture just until blended; don't over mix.

Add the zucchini and stir until evenly distributed throughout batter. Add the 3/4 cup chocolate chips and stir.

Scrape into loaf pan. Sprinkle remaining chocolate chips on top.

Bake for about an hour, until a toothpick inserted into center comes out mostly clean. It might have some melted chocolate chips on it, but there should not be any runny batter, only a couple crumbs, if that.

Let cool in pan for 15 minutes or so, then ease out (use a spatula or knife around the edges to help, if needed) to finish cooling on a rack.

You don't have to keep chips out for the top if you don't want to; you can mix them all in.

Try it with 1/2 cup chopped nuts. Or with peanut butter, caramel, white chocolate, mint, or butterscotch chips instead of chocolate.

You can also skip mix-ins entirely, and just have a chocolate loaf with no chips or nuts.

Lemon Bread

1/2 cup (1 stick) butter, soft

1 cup sugar

2 eggs

1 ½ cups flour

1 tsp baking powder

1/2 tsp salt

1/2 cup milk

2 T lemon zest OR 2 ½ tsp dried lemon peel (half is for bread and half for glaze)

1 cup powdered sugar

3 T lemon juice (1 for bread, 2 for glaze)

Preheat oven to 350 and grease a loaf pan.

Beat the sugar until it's creamy. Add the sugar and beat until well mixed and light and fluffy.

Sift together flour, baking powder, and salt. Gradually add to butter mixture, alternating with milk until just mixed.

Add in 1 T lemon juice and 1 T lemon rind. If you're adding any mix-ins, add now.

Scrape into loaf pan and bake until toothpick poked into center comes out clean, about 1 hour.

Cool completely on a wire rack or a clean kitchen towel.

To make glaze, mix 2 T lemon juice with powdered sugar and lemon rind. (If you're using fresh zest, you can sprinkle it on top afterwards; if dried, it's better mixed in.) Pour over the top of the bread, letting the excess run down the sides.

Pumpkin Bread

1 can pumpkin puree (If you are using the frosting that is the next recipe, keep out 2 T of the pumpkin puree to use for frosting.)
1 cup oil

4 large eggs

2 ½ cups sugar

2/3 cup water

3 1/3 cups flour

2 tsp baking soda

1 ½ tsp salt

1 tsp nutmeg

1 tsp cinnamon

1/4 tsp dried ginger

1/2 tsp cloves
1 cup nuts or chocolate chips (optional)

Preheat oven to 350. Grease 2 large or 3 smaller loaf pans.

In main mixing bowl, combine pumpkin, oil, eggs, water, and sugar. Mix well

In a second bowl, combine all dry ingredients except the nuts/chocolate chips, if you're using those.

Add dry ingredients to wet ingredients, a bit at a time, mixing between each addition.

Divide evenly between loaf pans.

Bake for about 50-80 minutes (large pans with deeper batter take longer), until skewer, toothpick, or knife inserted into the top comes out clean.

You can use 1 T pumpkin pie spice blend instead of individual spices, if you wish.

If you are making muffins instead, bake for 25 minutes and check with a skewer whether they are done.

Pumpkin Frosting

1/4 cup (1/2 stick) unsalted butter, softened

2 Tablespoons canned pure pumpkin puree

1/2 teaspoon ground cinnamon

1/2 teaspoon vanilla

3 cups powdered sugar

2 teaspoons half & half or milk

1/4 to 1/3 cup chopped pecans or walnuts, optional, for sprinkling on top

Cream the butter, pumpkin puree, cinnamon, and vanilla, blending well. Add powdered sugar a cup at a time, blending well after each addition. Add half & half or milk and blend well.

NOTE: This makes a very thick butter cream frosting. If you want a thinner, creamier frosting, add more half & half or milk until you get the desired consistency.

After frosting the cooled pumpkin loaf, sprinkle with chopped pecans or walnuts if desired.

Grandma P's Pumpkin Spice Bread

And here's a pumpkin spice quick bread; it does not contain pumpkin, only the pumpkin spices. It would be tasty with the pumpkin frosting described above.

3 ½ cups flour

3 cups sugar

3 tsp baking soda

3 tsp salt

3 tsp cinnamon

1 tsp nutmeg or ½ tsp cloves

1 cup vegetable oil

4 eggs

2/3 cups water

1 cup nuts or raisins, optional

Preheat oven to 325 and grease 2 loaf pans very well.

Sift all dry ingredients (except nuts and raisins, if you're using those) together in a large bowl.

Make a well in the center of the dry ingredients and pour all remaining ingredients in the well.

Mix thoroughly.

Fill half of the loaf pans (this means fill pans halfway).

Bake about 1¼ hours, until toothpick in center comes out clean.

Apple Bread 1 – with Applesauce

There are a couple ways to make apple bread; one is to make it similar to banana bread, with applesauce instead of the bananas and adding cinnamon. The other is to make a basic quickbread with chopped apples as the fruit. I'll put both in this book.

1 ¾ cups flour

2 tsp baking powder

1/2 tsp salt

2/3 cup sugar

1/3 cup oil or butter

2 eggs

1 cup unsweetened applesauce

2 tsp cinnamon

1/4 tsp ginger

Preheat oven to 350 and grease a bread pan.

Mix the flour, baking powder, and salt together in one bowl.

Mix the eggs, oil, applesauce, spices, and sugar together in another mixing bowl.

Add the dry ingredients and mix just until combined.

Pour into greased pan and bake for about 45 minutes, until lightly brown and a skewer inserted in center comes out mostly clean, with just a few crumbs and no batter. Let cool 10 minutes or so, then turn out onto a cooling rack or a clean towel. It will cool faster on the rack, but even just on a towel will be faster than staying in the hot pan.

You can combine the two recipes, adding a chopped apple to this bread as well as the applesauce.

Apple Bread 2 – Basic Quickbread with Chopped Apples

2 cups flour

1 cup sugar

2 tsp baking powder

1/4 tsp salt
2 cups finely chopped apples, peeled and cored. I like a tart, firm apple for this, like granny smith, but any will work

2 eggs

1/2 cup melted butter

2 T milk
1 tsp vanilla

1 tsp cinnamon

1/4 tsp ginger (optional)

Preheat oven to 350 and grease a loaf pan.

In one bowl, mix together flour, sugar, baking powder, salt, and spices.

In another, beat the eggs until foamy, then beat in the butter, milk, and vanilla.

Add the dry ingredients, mixing until the dry ingredients are moistened.

Scrape into loaf pan and bake for about an hour, until a toothpick stuck in the center comes out clean.

Remove and cool completely, removing from pan after it's cooled for 10 minutes or so. (Removing bread from the pan too early can mean it sticks and breaks, instead of coming out cleanly.)

Blueberry Bread (or whatever you want to put in instead of blueberries – tip for savory at the end)

2 cups flour

1 T baking powder

1/2 – 3/4 cup sugar

1 tsp salt

2 eggs

1/4 cup melted butter or cooking oil

1 cup milk

1 tsp vanilla

1 cup blueberries

Preheat oven to 350 and grease a loaf pan.

Mix flour, baking powder, salt, and sugar together.

In another bowl, mix egg, milk, oil, and vanilla.

Add dry ingredients to wet until blended thoroughly.

Fold in blueberries.

You can use any other kind of berries, if you prefer. If they are large berries (or other fruit) chop up before adding. Or you can try chocolate chips, cinnamon swirl, chopped peaches – any kind of mix-in.

For a savory quickbread, decrease sugar to 1 T and add herbs, cheese, and/or chopped vegetables as mix-ins.

Gingerbread Loaf

I like gingerbread, with a bit dollop of freshly whipped cream. It's as tasty in the cool fall and winter as zucchini bread is in the summer. Both are good year-round, but they just seem to fit different seasons better.

1/2 cup (1 stick) butter

1 cup sugar

2 eggs

3/4 cup boiling water

3/4 cup molasses

2 ½ cup flour

2 tsp baking soda

1/2 tsp salt

2 tsp powdered ginger

Preheat oven to 350. Grease a loaf pan or 9″ square baking pan. Loaf pans take longer to bake because the batter is deeper and needs longer to bake the center.

Cream butter, add sugar, and beat until light.

Add eggs and beat well.

Combine boiling water and molasses together, then beat into mixture.

In a separate bowl sift together flour, baking soda, salt, and ginger. Add to the wet ingredients and combine thoroughly.

Pour into the pan and bake 35-45 min, until toothpick comes out clean. A loaf pan might need an hour; check at 45 minutes and see how close it is to done. Cool in pan 10 minutes before turning onto a cooling rack or clean towel to cool completely.

Another Gingerbread

I had a copy of Fannie Farmer's cookbook (my dog chewed it up, and I haven't gotten a new one yet) and this recipe was derived from one in there. There are a dozen kinds of gingerbread in the book; gingerbread was believed to have medicinal qualities in the 19th century (and ginger does help soothe your stomach; I'm not sure if it still does so if it's in sweet bread form). I've made it multiple times and people always like it.

1 cup molasses

1/2 cup boiling water

2 ¼ cups flour

1 tsp baking soda

1 ½ tsp powdered ginger

1 tsp salt

4 T melted butter

Preheat oven to 350 and grease a baking dish or loaf pan.

Sift together dry ingredients.

Mix molasses and water together.

Add water-molasses mixture to dry ingredients and stir until blended.

Add melted butter and beat thoroughly, until color lightens a bit.

Pour into greased pan and bake until done; skewer inserted into center will come out clean. It should take about half an hour, depending on pan (longer for loaf, less for baking dish).

Grandma P's No Sugar (just molasses) Gingerbread

Another selection from paternal grandma's recipe box. Did I mention I very much like gingerbread? This one is not strongly flavored; you can increases spices if you want.

1/2 cup melted shortening (I use butter)

1 ¼ cups molasses

2 eggs, well beaten

2 ½ cups flour

1 tsp salt

1 ½ tsp baking soda

dash cinnamon and cloves

1/2 tsp ginger

3/4 cup hot water

Preheat oven to 350 and grease a 9×13 pan

Mix everything together. The only directions the recipe card gives for this are to add the hot water last of all.

When I make it, I follow the usual order of baking things, just in case. Sift together the dry ingredients and set aside. Blend the wet ingredients – since there's a specific instruction to add it last, don't include the water with the wet ingredients, wait to add it till the end. Combine dry with wet. For this recipe, add the water last.

Put into greased pan. If you wish, you can sprinkle a little sugar on top for texture.

Bake for 45 minutes or until done (clean toothpick test). Let cool, cut and serve with whipped cream.

Powder Biscuits

This is the recipe I use for biscuits. I like it a lot better than the biscuits that come in a can. It's amazing with butter and honey or fresh apple butter.

2 cups flour

3 tsp baking powder

1 tsp salt

1 stick butter

2/3 cups milk, maybe a couple T more.

Preheat oven to 425 and grease a cookie sheet.

Mix together flour, baking powder, and salt. Cut in butter; it's easiest to use a food processor, but you can use your hands, two knives, or a pastry cutter instead if you don't have one. Add milk, mixing until dough holds together but is not too sticky.

Turn dough out onto floured surface, knead lightly until sticks together. Roll out about half an inch thick.

Cut out biscuits; you can just cut into squares, or use a cookie cutter, or a jar lid or glass.

Place on cookie sheet and bake 12 to 15 minutes, until golden brown.

You can substitute in half wheat flour; you may need a smidge more milk if you do.

English Muffins

Hot, fresh English muffins taste amazing. They tend to one of the more expensive breads in the store. These are not hard to make, and are just as good and cheaper.

1 cup milk

1/4 cup warm water

1 ½ tsp salt

2 T sugar or 1 ½ T honey

3 T butter, oil, or shortening

1 package or 2 ¼ tsp of dry yeast

1 egg

4 cups all-purpose flour

1/2 cup corn meal

Scald the milk. To scald milk, heat it almost, but not quite, to boiling. Nowadays, this is a simple way of saying use very hot (but not boiling) milk. In older recipes, before pasteurization, scalding was how you made milk safe to use.

Combine hot milk with salt, sugar, and butter in a mixing bowl and stir together. Butter will melt in the hot milk. Let mixture cool to lukewarm instead of hot.

While that's cooling, dissolve yeast in water. Add a spoon of flour (for yeast food) and stir, then let yeast rest and prove.

Once milk is cooled to lukewarm, add yeast mixture to it. Do not add it while milk's still hot; it will kill the yeast.

Beat the egg and add to mixture.

Stir in 3 cups of flour, and mix everything together very well.

When it's smooth, turn it out onto a very clean, floured surface. This can be your tabletop, a large cutting board, or a pastry mat.

Knead last cup of flour into the dough. Oil the bowl and put the dough back into it. Cover with a clean dish cloth and let rise in a warm spot until it doubles its size.

Once dough has raised, turn it out onto your clean, floured surface again. Knead it again. Let it sit for a minute; this makes it easier to roll out.

While it's sitting, sprinkle half the cornmeal over a surface – a cookie sheet works well and keeps the cornmeal from going everywhere.

Roll out the dough about 3/8 inch thick. Cut it – the ring from a large mouthed canning jar works well, as does a cookie cutter, a biscuit cutter, or a cup or glass about 4 inches across.

Put the raw circles on the corn meal and sprinkle the rest of the corn meal over the top of them. Cover them with your clean dishcloth and let them rise until they double in height.

Oil (or spray with cooking spray) a griddle or cast-iron pan. Place it over low-medium heat and let warm up, then bake the muffins on it, about 8-12 minutes a side, depending on heat. Be sure heat is not too high, or the outsides will cook while the insides are not done.

Cut in half (you can use your fingers, but it's messier than a knife) and eat with butter and jam, honey, eggs, cheese or whatever topping you want. If you have more than you can eat, seal in a freezer bag and thaw as needed.

You can substitute out half the flour for wheat flour, if you want.

Scones

I love scones. This is the first scones recipe I made, and the one that started the addiction. Note that is it not as sweet as the 'scones' you get from American bakeries.

3 cups flour

1/2 tsp salt

5 tsp baking powder

1/2 cup sugar

3/4 cup cold butter

1 egg, beaten

1 cup milk

Preheat oven to 375 and grease a cookie sheet.

Mix flour, salt, baking powder, and sugar, in mixing bowl or in bowl of food processor.

Cut in butter, by hand or using a food processor. If you used a food processor, pour mixture into mixing bowl now.

If you are adding any mix-ins (see after recipe), add them here.

In small bowl or large measuring cup, beat together egg and milk. Add to flour mixture and stir in with a fork, just until moistened.

Turn out onto clean, lightly floured surface. Knead gently for 30 seconds.

Shape dough into three round shapes about 3/8 inch thick.

Cut rounds into slices, like a pie. You can place the entire round onto the plate together, or separate into triangles to place. Keeping together makes slightly higher scones with soft edges, as the dough raises more upwards. Separate ends up a little thinner and has crisper edges.

Bake 10-12 minutes, until golden brown. Serve with jam and butter or clotted cream (recipe in sauces).

This makes plain scones; you can do a lot of things to them for variety and differing flavors. Try adding 1/4 to 1/2 cup of dried currents, blueberries, chocolate chips, raisins, chopped nuts, cranberries, and so on before mixing in the milk and egg. Or add shredded cheese, or chopped herbs, or different spices.

Bannock

A bannock is an egg-free quickbread that you can either bake or cook in a skillet, turning once halfway through. You can skip the butter/oil for oil free as well, but it tastes a little better with the butter. It originated and Scotland, and spread around all over Europe and America, so there are many variations on the recipe.

3 cups flour

2 T baking powder

1 ½ tsp salt

1/2 cup oil or softened butter

1 ½ cups water or milk

Preheat oven to 425 and grease a 9×9 baking pan or prepare a large skillet by greasing it.

Mix dry ingredients together. Make a well in the center and add wet ingredients; mix and knead them for 5 minutes, until well blended and not sticky.

Spread in baking dish and bake for 20 minutes, checking at 15 for done-ness. OR

Spread in cast-iron skillet or on a griddle and cook on top of stove (or over a campfire), turning when partway done. You can cook it in several smaller pieces, or all at once. Be sure you have space for turning it if you're cooking it in a skillet.

You can add sweeteners, spices, herbs, or chopped fruit for variations in flavor.

Popovers

I always thought popovers would be hard, but they really aren't. While you can use a proper popover pan (I found one at a thrift shop), you don't have to. They won't be as tall, but you can just use a muffin pan.

3 large eggs (can go 4 for a more egg-y taste)

1 ½ cups milk

1 ½ cups flour

1/2 tsp salt

3 T butter, cut into 12 equal pieces

Before preheating oven, check to see if you need to move the oven rack down a shelf; popovers rise a lot and you don't want the tops to scorch by being too close to a burner. I have a gas oven that heats from below, so I don't have to; my mom has an electric oven that heats above and below and she does.

Preheat oven to 450.

Grease muffin pan all over; not just in the cups, between them as well.

Beat eggs, then whisk in milk and salt until thoroughly blended and uniform in color.

Add flour all at once and mix until frothy. No large lumps should be there, but little ones are fine.

Pour into muffin tins, filling them about 2/3 to 3/4 full.

Drop a piece of butter in the center of each muffin of batter.

Bake for 20 minutes at 450. *Do not open the door. If you open the door they will not raise up high.*

Lower temperature to 350. Do not open the door. Bake for 10 to 15 minutes, until golden brown. If your oven doesn't have a window to look through, you can check quickly at 10 minutes.

Remove and eat immediately.

Popovers raise very high; the middles are hollow. You can open them up, once they're done, and put tasty things like jam, butter, or cream cheese filling in the hollow.

Corn Bread

Corn bread is delicious with butter and honey, or apple butter. It's great with a dish of beans, or a bowl of chili. It goes well with mashed potatoes, dinner loaf, and green beans. It's a good all-round accompaniment for all kinds of meals, or just as a meal in itself.

1 ¼ cups cornmeal

1 cup flour

1/3 cup sugar

1 T baking powder

1/2 tsp salt

1/4 cup oil or melted butter, slightly cooled

1 large egg, beaten lightly

1 cup milk

Preheat oven to 400 and grease an 8 inch square baking dish

Mix all dry ingredients together in mixing bowl.

In smaller bowl, mix together oil, egg, and milk.

Blend wet ingredients into dry ingredients, mixing just until moistened; some small lumps are normal.

Scrape into baking dish and smooth top with spatula.

Bake 20 to 25 minutes, until toothpick inserted into center comes out clean.

If I'm making the cornbread to have with jam or apple butter, I'll often add a tsp of vanilla and ½ tsp of cinnamon to it. It makes it taste sweet, without adding sugar.

Don't do this if you're making the cornbread to have with chili or beans; that just tastes odd. Some people even skip the sugar entirely if they're making it with a savory dish.

Soft Pretzels

I love a fresh mall pretzel, but they're not the cheapest (except in comparison with other mall food). They are just a kind of bread, though, and not difficult to make by pansfull at home.

3 tsp yeast (You can use less, then let it raise longer)
3/4 cup warm water or milk
2 tsp sugar

1 tsp salt

2 cups flour

2 T baking soda

1 cup Boiling water

2 T or so melted butter

Coarse salt, cinnamon sugar, Parmesan, or desired sprinkled seasoning.

Preheat oven to 425 and grease a cookie sheet or line it with parchment paper.

Mix yeast, sugar, salt, warm water, sugar, and flour together in a bowl.

Knead very well, at least 5 minutes constant kneading. Put in bowl and cover with plastic wrap, or put in large Ziploc bag, and let raise for half an hour at room temperature.

While dough is raising, combine baking soda and boiling water; stir until soda is completely dissolved. Remove from heat, pour into a baking dish for ease of dipping (8×8 should work) and let cool to lukewarm.

Divide the dough into 8-10 pieces.

Flour a clean, dry surface and roll out into thin ropes and twist into pretzel shapes. (Lay on surface in shape of a U; pick up the ends and twist twice, without lifting back of U off surface; fold ends back up to the back of the U and press into place.)

Dip pretzels into baking soda water, a few at at time. Let them soak for 2 minutes in the water, spooning or brushing it over any parts out of water, turn them over halfway through to ensure complete coating.

Remove from water and put pretzels on the cookie sheet, repeat with next batch of pretzels.

Let raise a 10 minutes. You can sprinkle on salt here, if you want, or wait until after they bake and sprinkle on after you butter them. (I wait)

Bake until golden brown, about 13-15 minutes.

Remove from oven and brush with butter, then sprinkle with salt, cinnamon sugar, or other seasoning.

These are really good with the cheese sauce listed in sauce chapter; you can make a full batch of the sauce and use half for another dish (over broccoli) or just make a half batch.

Desserts

Ah, desserts. The part of meals that I find the most fun to cook. I like baking. I like eating desserts. I have a lot of family and friends that like for me to bake desserts, and give them away because I made too much.

Delicious, but not usually the most healthy, what with the sugar, butter, and more use of refined flours than the other baked goods. Read the ingredients; some of these might surprise you. Fruit fool is surprising low sugar (though not low fat).

There are things you can do to make them less bad – reduce sugar, use half whole grain flour, choose desserts that have fruit. But still, even if they're delicious, eat in moderation, as part of an overall more-balanced and healthy eating style.

Basic Cake Recipe

This is a basic cake recipe that I think tastes much better than most bought mixes or premade cakes. It's firm and a little dense, and holds its shape well. It makes 1 layer, 8 inch square or 9 inch round. Double it if you want to make a layer cake. While still sweet, it has less sugar than most bought cakes and mixes, and no preservatives or unwanted chemicals. Be sure not to make more cake than you'll eat in a few days; it does go stale faster without the chemicals.

1 ½ cups flour.

1/2 tsp salt

2 tsp baking powder

1/2 cup (1 stick) unsalted butter, softened

3/4 cup granulated sugar
1 tsp vanilla

2 eggs, room temperature

3/4 cup milk, room temperature

Preheat oven to 350. Grease the cake pan and line bottom with parchment paper (you can dust the bottom of the pan with flour instead, but the paper works better in preventing sticking).

Sift dry ingredients together in a bowl.

Cream together the butter and sugar until they are light and fluffy. Don't skimp on this; the sugar/butter mix will be lighter in color and have no lumps.

Add the vanilla.

Add the eggs, 1 at a time, mixing thoroughly each time.

Add a little flour, a little milk, alternating back and forth until they are both completely added.

Pour into cake pan and bake until done, about 30 minutes. To check for done-ness, lightly tap the top of the cake; if it bounces back, it's done.

You can use different flavorings if you want a different flavored cake – almond, mint, lemon.

You can fold in fruit at the end the mixing.

For chocolate cake, substitute 1/3 or so cup of cocoa for the same amount of flour. Or melt a couple square of baker's chocolate, let cool slightly, and mix into the batter with the wet ingredients.

If you are frosting it, basic buttercream is good. I also like using cream cheese frosting with raspberry jam as a filling between layers. Or you can just used whipped cream.

Oatmeal Cake by Grandma P

My paternal grandma didn't know how to cook when she and grandpa got married, so she put a lot of work into learning and had a box of favorite recipes, collected on stained 3×5 cards. Her recipes (and Grandma B's, when I have them – she tended towards memory and cookbooks for her cooking) are scattered through this book.

1 cup rolled oats

1 stick oleo (I use butter)

1 ¼ cup boiling water

1 cup white sugar

1 cup brown sugar

2 eggs, beaten

1 ½ cup flour

1/2 tsp salt

1 tsp soda

1 tsp cinnamon

1 tsp nutmeg

Put oats and butter in a bowl; pour boiling water over them and let stand for 20 minutes.

Preheat oven to 350 and grease a 9×13 inch pan.

Mix all ingredients together.

Scrape into pan and bake for 40 minutes or until it passes the toothpick test. Allow to cool completely, then top with the coordinating frosting.

Coconut Nut Frosting for the Oatmeal Cake

This is a different kind of frosting; it's made hot and almost caramelized before you apply it, still warm, to the cake.

1/2 stick butter (1/4 cup) softened

1/2 cup sugar

1/2 cup milk

1/2 tsp vanilla

1 cup nuts, chopped

1 cup coconut

In a saucepan over low-med heat, melt together butter and sugar.

Add milk. bring to boil and boil for 1 minute. Remove from heat.

Add vanilla, nuts, and coconut and mix thoroughly.

Put on cake while still warm, then put cake under broiler and brown slightly.

Mocha Walnut Torte

This is an extremely rich dessert; when you slice it, cut small pieces.

9 oz chocolate chips

2/3 c. butter

1 cup walnuts (about 4 oz)

2 T flour

6 eggs lightly beaten

3/4 cup granulated sugar

1 tsp vanilla

2T hot water and 1 tsp instant coffee **or** 2T VERY strong coffee

Preheat oven to 350. Grease or line with parchment paper a 9 inch cake pan; a springform pan that disassembles around the cake when it's done is best.

Melt chocolate and butter together in a double boiler over simmering water, stirring occasionally, till smooth.

Grind walnuts and flour together in a food processor until very fine and well mixed.

Beat eggs, sugar, vanilla and coffee together for one full minute.

Slowly add chocolate and butter mix

Gradually blend in nut and flour mixture.

Pour into pan and spread evenly. Bake 25-35 minutes

Cool in pan for 15 minutes. Turn onto wire rack to cool fully.

Mocha Ganache

Melt 4 oz chocolate chips, 1/4 cup heavy cream, 1 T vanilla and 1 T strong coffee together in double boiler until smooth. Pour over fully cooled torte (or any other cake or pastry you desire). Garnish with candy, nuts, sprinkles etc. as you like.

Basic Brownie Recipe

1 cup butter

2 cups sugar

2 teaspoons vanilla extract

4 eggs

3/4 cup baking cocoa
1 cup all-purpose flour

1/2 teaspoon baking powder

1/4 teaspoon salt

1 cup chopped nuts(optional)

Heat oven to 350°F. Grease 13×9×2-inch baking pan.

Melt butter. Mix well with sugar and vanilla.

Add eggs, one at a time, beating well after each egg.

Add cocoa; beat until well blended.

Add flour, baking powder and salt; beat well. Stir in nuts, if desired.

Pour batter into prepared pan.

Bake 30 to 35 minutes or until brownies begin to pull away from sides of pan. Cool completely in pan on wire rack.

You can add chocolate chips if you want, instead of or in addition to nuts. Or peanut butter chips, butterscotch chips, etc.

If you like mint chocolate, you can chop up some mint leaves and mix them into batter. Or crush candy canes and mix in. Or substitute 1 tsp of mint flavoring for one of the tsp of vanilla.

If you want a really easy chocolate topping, spread chocolate chips on the top as soon as it comes out of the oven. Let it sit for minute until they are soft, then spread them out like frosting. Let cool. Try drizzling caramel topping over the hot chocolate chips, and using a toothpick pulled through to make designs on top.

This has a high sugar content, and I will often use only 1 to 1 1/2 cups of sugar, but that might make this not quite sweet enough for your tastes. Experiment and see what level of sweetness you like best.

Basic Pie Crust

2 sticks, or 1 cup, of butter, cut into half inch cubes.

2 ½ cups flour

1 tsp salt

1 tsp sugar, optional

6-8 T ice water

Be sure your butter is very cold; some people freeze it, but that makes it harder to work with.

Mix together flour, salt, sugar.

Add butter. There are a couple ways to get the butter mixed in with the flour in pie crust. If you have a food processor, just whiz them together in short bursts until they are coarsely blended – about the consistency of corn meal, with some pea-sized bits of butter still in. If you don't, then you rub the cubes of butter and the flour between your fingers until you reach the same point, or cut them in with two knives or a pastry cutter.

Slowly add ice water; you may not need it all. Knead in a tablespoon or so at a time, until the dough sticks together. Separate dough into two pieces, one piece a little larger than the other. The slightly larger piece is the lower crust, the other is the top. Divide into equal pieces if you are making two pies without a top crust. Wrap in plastic wrap, or put in a bowl and cover with a damp cloth, and chill in fridge for at least an hour.

When ready to use, remove from fridge and let rest a couple minutes. Place dough disk on clean, floured surface and roll out to about 1/8 inch thick. Check while rolling to be sure it's not sticking to the surface; sometimes I roll it on wax paper to be sure, and use that as a means by which to move the dough.

Carefully place in pie pan. Check to be sure pie pan is covered, and close off any holes with dough.

Fill with filling.

If making a double-crust pie, roll out top the same way. Crimp top and bottom together firmly, and slice some openings in the top to allow controlled escape of steam and reduce chances of pie making a mess in your oven. You could also use a pie bird (it's like a little chimney for your pie). Bake as directed by the filling recipe.

Tip: Put a pizza pan or cookie sheet under your pie to catch any drips that might happen.

Some recipes, like pumpkin pie and quiche, suggest that you **blind-bake** the crust. This simply means partially baking an empty crust before adding the filling. This helps prevent soggy crusts. You don't just bake an empty pie shell; the dough will bubble up and be bumpy. Place the crust in the pan, crimping the edges and ensuring it is solid and even. Line it with parchment paper, then fill it with dried beans, pie weights, or pennies. Bake for 15-20 minutes at 350, then remove. Take out the weights carefully – they are very hot. Let crust cool, add filling, and bake as directed.

Bonus: You can roll out any extra or left over pie crust (say, from trimming the edges all around) flat and put it on a cookie sheet. Use a pizza cutter or knife to mark it off in squares, and prick all over with a fork to let out air. Sprinkle top with salt and bake at 400 until crisp, but along the lines, and voila – you've made your own butter crackers. They'll be really crumbly, but taste great.

Cookie Crust, including Graham Cracker

The most common type of cookie crust is graham cracker. You can also use chocolate wafer, ginger snaps, vanilla wafers, or any kind of crispy cookie.

1 ½ cups crumbs (about 9 graham crackers worth)

6 T unsalted butter, melted

1/4 to 1/3 cup sugar, optional (not needed if you're using cookies, and I never use it with graham crackers either)

Grind the cookies or crackers to crumbs, either by running in a food processor, or by rolling over them with a rolling pin until they are crumbs. If using a rolling pin, it helps to put them in a Ziploc bag or put them in a cookie sheet to keep crumbs contained.

If using sugar, add it now.

Mix crumbs with butter until thoroughly blended. Put into pie pan and press firmly against bottom and sides of pan; you can use a fork or a cup to help be sure crust is even.

Optional: Bake at 375 for 7-9 minutes. I tend not to do this if it's a pudding pie, and will sometimes do it if it's fruit, or if I'm using a kind of cookie other than graham crackers. I always bake if I'm making a gingersnap crust for a peach icebox pie. I might not for a plain graham cracker crust for a strawberry pie.

Peach Icebox Pie (notes for other fruit)

1 Gingersnap crust (see recipe above)

5-6 fresh, ripe summer peaches

2 T granulated sugar

Prepare crust as directed, bake at 375 for 7-9 minutes, and let cool.

Peel and slice peaches. The best way to peel peaches is to blanch them. Get a pan of boiling water, a slotted spoon, and a bowl of ice water. Wash the peaches, score a small x on the bottom of each peach, then put them in the boiling water. Use spoon to turn them and submerge them so that all surfaces are hot. Heat peaches for 2-3 minutes, then scoop out into the ice water. Roll them around for minute to ensure all surfaces are shock-cooled. Using the small cuts as a starting point, simply pull the peels off. This is easier than using a knife, and wastes no peach flesh. Cut peach in half around pit, twist gently so that halves separate, and remove pit. Cut into slices and put into a bowl. When all peaches are sliced, mix them with the sugar to lessen browning from air contact.

You can put whipped topping on top, chill for at least an hour, and call it a day – that is the cheapest way. Or make the delicious cream cheese whipped cream topping described in the next recipe. It tastes fantastic with this.

For other nonbaked fruit pies, wash, peel (if needed), and slice the fruit. Use soft fruits, like strawberries, other berries, nectarines, or soft pears. Toss with sugar, put in crust – graham cracker or cookie – and cover with some kind of topping to protect from the air. Then chill, covered, for at least 2 hours before serving.

Cream Cheese Whipped Cream Topping

1 package of cream cheese, room temperature.

1 pint of heavy whipping cream

1/2 cup powdered sugar

1/2 tsp vanilla

Whip the cream cheese, vanilla, and sugar together until it is light and fluffy.

Add about a quarter of the whipping cream and beat well. Scrape sides of bowl to be sure it is all blending together, then add another quarter of the whipping cream, mix well, scrape. Repeat for the remaining two portions of whipping cream.

You can use other flavorings if you want something different than vanilla to match your filling – try 1 tsp dried lemon peel, or 1/4 tsp cinnamon, or 1/2 tsp mint extract.

For use on a fruit pie, like the peach one above, spread thickly over the top of the fruit, so that none of the fruit is exposed to air, and chill for a couple of hours before serving.

You can use this topping as a fruit dip. You can put it between cookies to make sandwiches. You can use it to frost a cake, or mix in streaks of fruit preserves and serve as a kind of pudding.

Apple Pie

1 pie crust, top and bottom

6 cups apples, peeled, cored, and sliced medium thin. (7 or so apples, depending on size) Use a firm, tart apple, like Granny Smith, Fuji, or Winesap.

3 T flour

1/3-1/2 cup granulated sugar

1 tsp cinnamon

1/2 tsp ground ginger

1/4 tsp nutmeg, optional

Preheat oven to 375.

Roll out pie crust and put lower crust in 9 inch pan. If you are using a pie bird, place it now.

In large bowl, mix together flour, sugar, and spices. Toss apples in mix, being sure they are coated thoroughly.

Put apples in pie, spreading evenly, maybe heap a little higher in the center for a really full pie.

Roll out top crust and stretch over pie. Cut off extra; do this by running a sharp knife along the edge of the pie plate. Once extra is off, crimp or press all along pie plate to be sure top and bottom are joined thoroughly. Make slices in top crust for steam or escape. You might also roll the top crust out, cut it into strips, and weave them on top of pie for a lattice look.

Bake for 45 minutes to an hour, until crust is golden brown and apples are softened.

Options: Some people add a tablespoon of butter, cut into small pieces and scattered over the filling before the top crust is added. I think it depends how juicy your apples are; dry apples might need it, but most nicely juicy ones don't. You can also brush the crust with beaten egg white before baking; this makes it look shiny once it's baked.

Basic Fruit Filling

I'm making this today, using frozen mixed berries. It can be used to make a baked pie filling with most kinds of fruit.

One double-crust pie crust

6 cups fruit

1 T lemon juice (not needed for all kinds of fruit, but tasty with most)
3 T flour

1/2 to 1 cup sugar

1 T butter, cut into small pieces (optional)

Spices, if desired.

I won't be using spices with the berries, but I'm going to make a firm pear pie for Christmas that will be seasoned with nutmeg.

Mix together flour and sugar

Toss fruit with flour mixture.

Put into pie crust, and dot with small bits of butter.

Put top crust on and slice ventilation slices.

Bake at 350 for 45 minutes or so, until crust is golden and filling is cooked through.

Mix and Match Pumpkin Pie

This is a basic pumpkin pie recipe. There are a lot of variations. Read the recipe carefully; it's written in a way to give you several options at different points.

Prepare a batch of pie crust. You'll only need the bottom crust, so you can either make a half recipe, make 2 pies, or wrap half of the dough thoroughly and refrigerate for up to two weeks to use later.

1 can pumpkin (15 ounces)

1 can sweetened condensed milk

OR

1 can evaporated milk (or 1 1/2 cups half and half) and 1/2 cup packed brown sugar, 1/3 cup white sugar

2 large eggs

1/2 tsp salt

1 T pumpkin pie spice blend

OR

1 ½ tsp cinnamon, 1/2 tsp ground ginger, 1/2 tsp allspice, 1/4 tsp nutmeg, 1/8 tsp cardamom

1 tsp vanilla, optional and/or 1/2 tsp dried lemon peel

Blind bake the crust. (Not absolutely necessary, but makes firmer crusts.)

Preheat oven to 425

Make the filling:

Beat the pumpkin to be sure there aren't any fibers left from processing.

Mix together eggs, sugars, spices. Add milk, if not already included.

172

Add pumpkin to mix and beat well.

Pour into pie crust and bake for 15 minutes, then lower temperature to 350 and bake for 45 to 55 minutes. Pie is done when knife inserted into center comes out wet but mostly clean; center will be a little bit jiggly, but otherwise firm.

Allow to cool completely and serve with whipped cream.

You'll notice there are options under the milk, the sweeteners, and the spices. There are dozens of pumpkin pie recipes out there; this lets you choose what you like best. The simplest is just five ingredients – premade pie crust, pumpkin, sweetened condensed milk, eggs, and premixed pie spice. Or you can get more elaborate and use individual sugar, dairy, or spices to your own taste. If you want to get even more elaborate, you can prepare your own pumpkin or Hubbard squash and go from there. Find your pumpkin pie happy place, and enjoy.

Chocolate Chip (or other insertions!) Cookies

1 cups (2 sticks) butter, room temperature

1 cup brown sugar

1 cup white sugar

2 eggs

2 tsp vanilla

3 cups flour

1 tsp baking powder

1 tsp salt

1 bag chocolate chips

1 cup chopped nuts, optional

In large bowl, beat butter until creamy. Add sugars, eggs, and vanilla and beat until light and fluffy.

In a different bowl, mix together flour, baking powder, and salt.

Add dry ingredients to wet ingredients, a quarter at a time. Mix until well blended.

Add chocolate chips and nuts, if desired.

Cover and put in the refrigerator to chill for at least two hours.

Grease a cookie sheet, two if you have two so that you can change pans with less down time. You can line the cookie sheets with parchment paper instead, if you like.

Put by rounded tablespoonfuls (basically 2 T) on the cookie sheet. Bake for 11-15 minutes, until edges are done and tops are not shiny.

Remove pan. If you have a second one ready to go, put it in now. Wait 7 or so minutes for cookies to cool slightly before removing from pan and putting on either a cooling rack or a clean, lint-free kitchen towel-lined surface to finish cooling.

Options:

You can cut the sugar by up to a third, if you want less sweet cookies.

You don't have to use chocolate chips; you can use butterscotch chips, white chocolate chips and macadamia nuts, a mix of different kinds of chips, or dried fruit.

Make cranberry-lemon cookies instead: try substituting lemon juice for one or both of the spoons of vanilla, adding 1/2 tsp of dried lemon peel, with cranberries instead of chocolate chips.

If you don't have chocolate chips, or want larger chunks, you can chop up a candy bar or two and use that instead.

For slightly crisper cookies, takes out 1/4 cup of flour and replace it with 1/4 cup of corn starch.

You can substitute in maple syrup for some of the sugar, if desired. Not all, as the extra liquid will make the batter runny. (If you really want to use only maple, there is maple sugar, or you can decrease the milk.)

Sugar Cookies

1 cup butter (2 sticks), room temperature

1 cup granulated sugar

1 ½ tsp vanilla or almond flavoring
1 egg

3 cups flour

1 tsp baking powder

3/4 tsp salt

In one bowl, mix together dry ingredients (flour, baking powder, salt) and set to the side.

In another large bowl, beat butter and sugar until creamy.

Add egg and flavoring and mix thoroughly.

Gradually add dry ingredients to butter mix until completely combined.

Chill in fridge for a couple hours.

Preheat oven to 375.

Grease a cookie sheet, two if you have two so that you can swap pans with less down time. You can line the cookie sheets with parchment paper instead, if you like.

Flour a flat, clean, dry surface. Take a manageable piece of dough – maybe about softball size – and roll it out a quarter inch thick.

Cut with cookie cutter and put on cookie sheet.

Bake for 10-12 minutes, until edges are just starting to turn golden brown.

Let cool on cookie sheet until they are firm enough to transfer to a cooling surface to cool completely.

Don't try to put icing on hot cookies; it will melt right off.

I usually use buttercream frosting on cookies; it tastes better than other kinds I've tried. It's the same one I make for cakes.

You can also just sprinkle colored sugar on the tops of the cookies before you put them in the oven; they'll bake in, and you can skip frosting entirely if you want.

Buttercream Frosting

1 stick butter, softened

3 cups powdered sugar

1 ½ tsp vanilla (or whatever flavoring you like)
1-2 T milk

Beat the butter until light and fluffy. Add the vanilla.

Gradually mix in sugar.

Add milk a little bit at a time, only until frosting is as soft as you intend. Too much, and it's runny. You can correct that by adding more sugar, but if you keep that up too long (too much milk, add sugar; too much sugar, add milk) it ends up not quite right. Also, you end up with a lot of frosting left over.

Use on cookies, cakes, cupcakes, or other frosting-requiring desserts.

For chocolate buttercream, substitute 1/2 cup unsweetened cocoa for 1/2 cup of the powdered sugar.

Keep leftovers refrigerated in a tightly sealed container to use on a later dessert.

Layered Bar Cookies

1 1/2 cups graham cracker crumbs

1/2 cup (1 stick) butter, melted

1 (14-ounce) can sweetened condensed milk (NOT evaporated milk)

1 cup butterscotch-flavored chips

1 cup semi-sweet chocolate chips

1 1/3 cups flaked coconut

1 cup chopped nuts

Preheat oven to 350 degrees F (325 degrees F for glass baking pan). Line a 13×9 inch baking pan (including sides) with a sheet of aluminum foil. Coat foil lightly with no-stick cooking spray. You can also use parchment paper.

In small bowl, combine graham cracker crumbs and butter; mix well. Press crumb mixture firmly on bottom of 13×9-inch baking pan.

Layer chips, coconut and nuts evenly over crust.

Drizzle condensed milk evenly over top of everything.

Bake 25 minutes or until lightly browned. Cool.

Lift up edges of foil to remove from pan. Cut into individual squares. Lift off of foil.

Thumbprint Cookies

These are unexpectedly delicious. They're also small. I have to be careful when making them, because suddenly half a dozen are gone and I have crumbs on lips.

1 cup unsalted butter, softened

1/4 cup granulated sugar

1 teaspoon pure vanilla extract

2 cups all-purpose flour

1/4 teaspoon salt

1 cup pecans, toasted and finely chopped

1 ¼ cups confectioners' sugar

2 tablespoons plus 2 teaspoons whole milk

Food coloring

Beat butter and granulated sugar together until they are white and fluffy. Add vanilla.

Gradually mix in flour, salt, and pecans.

Wrap in plastic, and refrigerate until firm, about 1 hour.

Preheat oven to 325. Line cookie sheets with parchment paper (it works better than greasing in this recipe; you can try just greasing if you don't have parchment paper. They'll stick a little.)

Shape dough into 1 1/4-inch balls, and space 2 inches apart on parchment-lined baking sheets. Press thumb into center of each cookie to make a little depression (you'll be filling that with icing later).

Bake 10 minutes. Remove from oven; press centers with the end of a wooden spoon to deepen depression and make room for icing (it will have raised up a bit).

Return to oven and bake longer, until golden brown, about 10 to 15 minutes.

Remove from oven and let cool completely before removing from cookie sheets.

Stir together confectioners' sugar and milk; tint with food coloring. Fill hollow centers of cookies with icing.

Let set overnight.

Cookies can be stored in airtight containers up to 1 week.

You can decorate with drizzles of opposite color almond bark or sprinkles, if desired.

Keep them refrigerated.

Gingerbread Cookies

These are delicious; I just decorate with buttercream, because I think the flavors blend well. These aren't the same recipe you'd use for making a gingerbread house – that's a different recipe with more flour and is designed for solidity rather than eating pleasure. These have a nice texture as well as flavor.

3/4 cups butter

3/4 cup brown sugar

3/4 cup molasses

1 egg
1 tsp salt

2 tsp cinnamon

2 tsp ground ginger

1/4 tsp cloves or allspice

1/2 tsp nutmeg

1 tsp baking powder

1/2 tsp baking soda

3 ½ cups flour

You can either melt the butter and let it cool, or beat it until light and fluffy. Melted butter means denser cookies, beaten makes lighter cookies.

Beat in the sugar, molasses, spices, salt, and egg. If you melted the butter, add the egg last, so that it is cool enough not to cook the egg instead of having it mix in smoothly.

Whisk flour, baking powder, and baking soda together.
Add flour mixture to wet ingredients gradually until it is all mixed in.

Wrap dough well and put in refrigerator to chill for 3 hours. If you don't completely chill the dough, it will lose its shape when you bake the cut outs and instead of gingerbread men, trees, wreathes, or whatever, you'll have gingerbread blobs. Still tasty, but not looking like anything in particular. While you're chilling things, it helps to chill your rolling pin. I stick mine in the freezer for an hour; my mom just keeps her rolling pin in her freezer.

When the dough is ready, flour a clean, dry surface and preheat oven to 350. Line two cookie sheets with parchment paper.

Get a softball-sized piece of dough sit it on the floured surface, sprinkle a little bit of flour over the top so it doesn't stick to your rolling bin (or use a pastry cloth or wax paper for the same reason), and roll it out to about 1/4 inch thick. Thinner dough is crisper cookies, thicker is chewier cookies. I tend to go thicker, especially if I'm frosting them. Keep the dough you're not directly working with chilled.

Bake for about 10 minutes, until the edges brown a little and cookies are firm. Time will vary depending on how large the shapes are that you're baking. Let cool on the sheets for 5 minutes, then move to rack or clean towel-covered surface to cool completely.

Continue until all dough is used up. You can ball up the scraps from between the shapes and roll them out again to cut.

Feel free to tinker with the spices. You can season with only cinnamon and ginger if you don't want other spices. You can increase the ginger, if you like really zingy cookies. Some don't use nutmeg at all; some use mace instead for a lighter flavor. Some people add some ground black pepper for extra bite, or cardamom just because, or vanilla to sort of soften the edges of the flavors.

No Molasses Gingerbread Cookies

These have a milder flavor, with no molasses and fewer spices.

1 cup butter, softened

2 cups packed brown sugar

3 eggs

2 tsp lemon zest (or 2/3 tsp dried lemon peel)

3 cups flour

1 tsp baking soda

1 tsp ground ginger

Cream butter and brown sugar in one bowl, until light and fluffy. Add the eggs and lemon peel and mix until thoroughly combined.

In another bowl, sift together the flour, baking soda and ginger.

Add to butter mixture gradually and mix well. It will be kind of sticky.

Wrap or cover and refrigerate for at least two hours; you'll know it's cold enough when it's easy to handle and the stickiness is a lot less.

Preheat oven to 350 and get out cookie sheets. Do not grease them; you can line them with parchment paper if you wish.

Flour a clean, dry surface. Roll out dough to 1/8-in. thickness and cut with small (about 2 inches) cookie cutters.

Place 2 in. apart cookie sheets. Bake for 8-10 minutes or until golden brown.

Let cool a few minutes, then remove to wire racks or a clean towel-covered surface to cool.

No Butter Frosting

1 ½ cups confectioners' sugar

1/2 teaspoon vanilla extract

2 to 3 tablespoons half-and-half or heavy cream

In a bowl, combine confectioners' sugar, vanilla and enough cream to achieve spreading consistency. Add the cream slowly, a tiny bit at a time; too much makes runny frosting that won't dry well. Add food coloring to some or all, if you wish, and frost cookies.

Vanishing Oatmeal Raisin Cookies

Another one from Grandma P's cards.

1 cup butter, softened

1 cup brown sugar

1/2 cup white sugar

2 eggs

1 ½ tsp vanilla

1 tsp cinnamon

1/2 tsp salt

1 ½ cups flour

1 tsp baking powder

3 cups oatmeal (rolled oats, not instant to steel-cut)

1 cup raisins

Preheat oven to 350 and get out cookie sheets. Do not grease them, though you can line them with parchment paper if you want.

Sift together flour, cinnamon, salt, baking soda.

Combine butter and sugars, beating until light and fluffy.

Add eggs and vanilla and combine thoroughly.

Mix in flour mixture.

Add oats and raisins and ensure everything is well combined.

Drop by tablespoonfuls onto cookie sheets.

Bake 10-12 minutes, or until golden brown.

Let cool 1 minute, then remove from cookie sheet and lay on clean towel to cool completely.

You can make this into bar cookies instead, if you like.

Press dough into an unreleased 9×13 metal baking pan. Bake for 30-35 minutes at 350. Cool completely before cutting.

Grandma P's Walnut Chews

2 sticks butter (1 cup)

2 cups brown sugar

2 eggs

2 tsp vanilla

2 cups flour

1/2 tsp baking soda

1/2 tsp salt

2 cups oatmeal

2 cups chopped walnuts

Chocolate chips (optional – recipe comments that "chocolate chips may be added", but why wouldn't you?)

Preheat oven to 350 and grease a 9×13 inch pan.

Cream together butter and sugar.   Beat in eggs and vanilla

Add flour, baking soda and salt. (I sift them together first.)

Stir in the oatmeal and walnuts. Add chocolate chips, if you're using them (amount up to you; I'd use a heaping cupful.

Spread in prepared pan and bake for 30-35 minutes.

Cream Cheese Frosting

I like this on cakes. It's really good on a yellow cake with raspberry jam, or on a spice cake or carrot cake.

1 package cream cheese

1 stick butter

1 pound (1 bag) powdered sugar

3 tsp vanilla

Beat cream cheese and butter together until light and fluffy.

Slowly add the powdered sugar. If you add too much at once, it will make a cloud of sugar that gets all over everything instead of mixing in well, so easy does it.

Add the vanilla.

Beat until well blended, light, and fluffy. Keep refrigerated, but let come to room temperature before trying to spread it.

Coconut Macaroons Two Ways

There are two main ways to make coconut macaroons; one uses condensed milk, and one uses egg whites. I greatly prefer the egg white ones, – they're crispy and lighter, and also what my mom made every Christmas – so that's the recipe I'm listing first. They are crumblier and crisper than the condensed milk ones. They're also easier to make a half-batch of; the other recipe means you have to find some way to use up the rest of the can of condensed milk. With these, you have egg yolks left to use – you can add them to other cookies for richness, or save them to make a hollandaise sauce (so delicious!).

With Egg Whites

2 cups shredded, dried coconut

2 egg whites

1/2 cup sugar

1/4 tsp salt

Preheat oven to 375 and grease or line a cookie sheet with parchment paper. (Paper's best, as these tend to stick.)

Beat egg whites with salt until they reach the soft peak stage. (When you lift out beaters, eggs form frothy peaks.)

Add sugar a tablespoon at a time and beat until glossy.

Fold in coconut with a spatula and mix gently with the spatula until well blended.

Drop onto cookie sheet by teaspoonfuls.

Bake until golden brown, about 12 minutes.
Let cool completely, on rack or clean towel covered surface.

With Condensed Milk

These ones are sturdier; you can dip them in melted chocolate, and they ship better if you're sending them away as a gift. Maybe you don't want to figure out what to do with the egg yolks. Or just like how they taste better. This recipe makes a much larger batch of macaroons, because you need to use up the whole can of condensed milk.

5 ½ cups dried shredded coconut, packed firmly

2 tsp vanilla

1/2 tsp salt

1 can condensed milk (that's the sweetened one; don't get it mixed up with evaporated milk)

Preheat oven to 325 and grease or line cookie sheets with parchment paper.

Combine everything thoroughly in a bowl.

Scoop by rounded teaspoonfuls onto cookie sheets., leaving 1 1/2 inches between them.
Bake for 10-12 minutes, until golden brown. Cool on wire racks or clean, towel-covered surface.

Make Your Own Instant Hot Chocolate

Here are two ways to let you make your own powdered hot chocolate. To one you add hot milk, to the other you only need hot water. You can experiment with the proportions. Don't use a whole recipe; cut it down, keeping proportions between the ingredients the same, until you find the level of sweetness, chocolate, and milk that tastes bests to you. These end up being much less per cup then the instant packets you get in the store.

Add milk:

3 cups powdered sugar

1 cup cocoa powder, preferably dark or Dutch processed

1 tsp salt

Sift all ingredients together at least three times, to remove lumps and to ensure complete blending.

To use, add 1/4 cup mix to 3/4 cup hot milk, stirring well.

If you prefer less sweet hot chocolate, try 2 to 1 sugar/cocoa instead of 3 to 1. If you like it sweeter, go 4 to 1. I like even less sweet, so I'll go 1 to 1.

With powdered milk included, so you just add water:

2 cups powdered milk (not nondairy creamer; that is a very different thing)
2 cups powdered sugar
1 cup cocoa powder

1-2 tsp cornstarch (optional, helps keep it from clumping)
1 tsp salt

Thoroughly blend all ingredients, running through a sieve, or even a blender or food processor.

Add 2-3 T to 8 oz hot water (or more to taste); for best blending, add mix to a couple tablespoons of water and mix it up, then add the rest of the hot water

For either, store tightly sealed in a jar. You can divide it into several jars, with different add-ins for each jar. Or give jars as gifts.

Optional add-ins:
White chocolate chips or chopped bits

Chocolate chips or chopped chocolate bars

Mini marshmallows

Pinch of chili powder

Drop of vanilla when you're mixing up a cup. Or make vanilla sugar and use that for some of the sugar.

Ground candy canes

Instant coffee

My Favorite Hot Chocolate

My husband prefers the instant mixes, but this is my favorite. You make it up one cup at a time; it's rich, thick, and filling. It's not instant, and takes attention throughout cooking to get right. It feels luxurious, but doesn't actually cost much. I sent it in to Chocosphere, and they put it in their newsletter.

1 cup whole milk

2 squares unsweetened bakers chocolate

Sugar to taste

Flavorings (based on mood – a drop of vanilla, pinch of chili, spoon of instant coffee, stir with a candy cane, etc.)

Heat milk on the stove. Do no boil, but bring to simmer, until it's steaming.

Remove from heat and let sit for a few minutes. A skin will form on the top; carefully remove this skin with a spoon. (I don't always do this step, but it does make a difference in texture and flavor.)

Return to very low heat. Break up chocolate and put in. Do not allow to boil, but stir continuously as the chocolate melts.

Continue to stir as chocolate and milk blend completely – no little specks of chocolate, a smooth, uniform color.

Add the amount of sugar you think you'll want, and flavoring – if not sure, estimate low. It's easy to add a pinch more if you need it.

Heat and stir for a full five minutes after chocolate is melted and blended. This is kind of like the conching that chocolate gets as it's processed from beans to bars. (A conche is a surface scraping mixer and agitator that evenly distributes cocoa butter within chocolate, and may act as a "polisher" of the particles.) This continual stirring is what gives this chocolate it's amazing texture and mouthfeel. I've

194

skipped this step before, and it really does make a huge difference in smoothness and taste.

Pour into a cup and drink. It should have the consistency of tomato soup. It's great for dipping cookies in. This is rich enough I often end up saving some for later because I get full; it's not quite as good reheated, but is still tasty. You can top with whipped cream if you want.

Date Bars

This, along with the coconut macaroons, were my Dad's favorite Christmas cookies Mom would make when we were kids.

3 cups chopped, pitted dates

1 ½ cups water

1/4 cup sugar

1 cup packed brown sugar

1 cup butter, softened

1 ¾ cups flour

1 ½ cups quick oats

1/2 tsp baking soda

1/2 tsp salt

In a saucepan, combine the dates, water, and sugar. Cook over low heat until thickened, stirring constantly; it takes about 10 minutes. Remove from heat and let cool completely,

Preheat oven to 400 and grease a 9×13 baking dish.

Beat sugar and butter together.

Add flour, oats, baking soda, and salt. Blend well.

Press half of the crust mixture in the baking dish, pressing firmly and evenly.

Spread the filling mixture over the crust.

Crumble the rest of the crust mixture evenly over the top. Press it lightly.

Bake for 25 to 30 minutes, until golden brown.

Let cool completely before cutting into bars.

Fruit Crisps or Crumbles

Crisps use oatmeal in their topping; crumbles use other add-ins like nuts, coconut, cornmeal – but no oats.

I've made this with a variety of fruits, depending what's in season or what I've got frozen. I'll switch up the seasonings between fruits (apples get cinnamon and ginger, mulberries got vanilla and cardamom, blueberries a touch of lemon, cherries plain), but the basic recipe remains the same. I think it will work with almost any bakeable fruit (it doesn't work well with citrus fruit or tropical fruit like bananas and mangoes), but I haven't tried everything yet.

Filling:

6 cups of chopped fruit (unless its small fruit like blueberries; they don't need chopped) If you're using frozen fruit, thaw it out.

1 T cornstarch

1 T lemon juice

Any filling seasonings you're using (1 tsp of vanilla, or 1 tsp of cinnamon, or 1/2 tsp of ginger, etc.)

1/4 to 3/4 cup sugar, depending on the tartness of the fruit (rhubarb needs more, ripe peaches would hardly need any)

Topping:

1/2 cup brown sugar

1/2 cup butter

1 cup flour

Any topping seasonings your using (cinnamon, nutmeg, etc.)

1 1/2 cup rolled oats for crisp

OR for a crumble, you can add nothing, just go with flour, butter, and sugar, or mix in 1/2 to 1 cup chopped nuts, coconut, or other add in

Heat oven to 375 and grease a 9×9 baking dish.

In large bowl, toss the fruit with cornstarch, lemon juice, and seasonings. (If you don't have corn starch, use 1/4 cup white flour.)

Spread fruit in pan.

Using hands of food processor, rub together butter, flour, sugar, and any spices until it's thoroughly blended and crumbly.

Mix in the oats (or other add ins) until well blended.

Spread topping evenly over top the fruit.

Bake for 35 minutes, or until fruit is bubbly and top is golden brown.

Fruit Fool

I love this; it's light and cool in summer, when the berries and fresh fruits are ripe and perfect for using. It's an old, old recipe, showing up referenced in the 16th century. It's simple, not too sweet, and uses fresh fruit.

1 ½ cups fresh fruit

1-2 T sugar

1 cup heavy whipping cream

2 T sugar

1/2 tsp vanilla

Chop the fruit and mix with the sugar. Let stand ten minutes, then run through a blender. You can keep half a cup out, for chunks of fruit, if you want; if you do that, mix blended and chopped fruit together and chill.

Whip the cream, sugar, and vanilla until almost-stiff peaks form.

Fold the fruit in gently, so that it makes fruit swirls through the cream.

This works great with soft fruits, like berries and peaches. If you're using a harder fruit, you'll need to cook and cool it before adding to the cream.

You can make it with rhubarb, and it's delicious, but you'll need to use more sugar. Mix 1 ½ cups chopped rhubarb, 1/3 cup sugar, 1 T water and simmer together until it's soft. Blend, cool thoroughly, and swirl through the whipped cream.

Breakfast

Just because this chapter is labeled breakfast doesn't mean you can't eat these foods other times, or that other foods are not fair game for breakfast. They're grouped here because in the area in which I live, when I think of pancakes or French toast, breakfast is the meal they fit. If I have pancakes for supper, it feels a little odd. They're still delicious, though.

There are a wide variety of breakfast foods. Some are very stereotypically breakfast, like French toast. Others can be had for a light supper, or as a part of another meal – bread pudding, quiche. Some are really fast to prepare, and others can take a while – really, some need planned the night before.

Making your own breakfast foods is cost effective and is better nutrition; I guarantee you that even if you put in chocolate chips, oatmeal is better for you than pop-tarts. In my opinion, it also tastes way better.

Have fun experimenting and eating these not-only-for-breakfast foods, any time of the day.

You can use some of these recipes at other meals, but they generally fit most with what we think of as breakfast, so I'm including them here.

Basic Pancakes (with a lot of ideas for jazzing them up)

There are a ton of ways to personalize these. I'll include a basic recipe, then several ways to alter it.

2 cups flour (I usually use one whole wheat and one white; adjust proportions as you like)
4 tsp baking powder

1 tsp salt

2 T sugar
2 large eggs

1/4 cup melted butter or oil

2 ½ cups milk

Mix together dry ingredients, then add wet ingredients and mix well. This makes a thin batter that makes somewhat thin pancakes; I'll suggest ways to change that after the recipe for if you want thicker pancakes.

Heat a lightly-greased frying pan on low to medium heat. I tend to use lower rather than hotter; too hot and the outsides will be overdone while the insides are still raw.

Pour batter on frying pan. Half-cups make an average sized pancakes, but you can use less for silver dollar pancakes, or kid pancakes, or more for larger pancakes.

Cook until edges look done and middle is bubbly, then flip pancake over and cook for a short time to finish that side. Repeat until all batter is used up.

Serve with desired toppings.

To thicken batter, there are two things I'll usually do. You can cut the milk by 1/2 to 1 cup. Or do as I usually do, and add a couple handfuls of rolled oats to the batter. Let it sit for 5 minutes to let the oats soak up some of the fluid, then cook. I like the texture and flavor this gives, and it makes you feel fuller for longer. Keep in mind that thicker batter will mean thicker pancakes, and you'll need to cook them longer to ensure the center is done.

To make these buttermilk pancakes, substitute 1 tsp of baking soda for one of the spoons of baking powder, and use buttermilk instead of regular milk. Buttermilk is not cheaper, but I find buttermilk powder in some groceries, and it is. Reconstitute it with water as per directions and use.

You can use reconstituted powdered or evaporated milk instead of fresh milk if milk is expensive right now where ever you live.

You can add inclusions to the batter for different flavors.

I'll often add a teaspoon or two of vanilla, and/or a teaspoon of cinnamon.

Add 1/2 to 1 cup of any of these: chocolate chips, chopped nuts, blueberries (dried or fresh), cranberries, chopped apples (good with cinnamon!), chopped strawberries, chopped peaches, chopped pears, vegetarian sausage.

Add 2-4 ripe mashed bananas for banana pancakes.

Butter and syrup are what most think of when thinking of pancakes, but it's far from the only option.

Try sprinkling brown sugar with butter instead of syrup, or use honey.

Peanut butter is great. Peanut butter and heated applesauce is delicious.

Use a fruit syrup or fruit soup as a topping, with or without peanut butter; recipes will follow the pancake recipes.

Just put dried or fresh fruit on top of your pancakes, again with or without butter and peanut butter.

Fruit Syrup

2 cups fruit

1/2-3/4 cup sugar

1/3 cup water

Prepare the fruit – wash well, peel, de-pit, remove leaves, whatever your fruit needs to be ready to eat. If it's a larger fruit like a peach or large strawberries, slice it up.

Put in a saucepan with the sugar and the water and bring to a simmer. Mash the fruit while it simmers – soft fruit like berries with mash easily, less soft fruit might need to simmer a few minutes. Mash, stir, and simmer until it looks thickened. Usually 5-10 minutes.

Now you have 3 options:

Serve as is, syrup with a few lumps of fruit is very good.

Run through a blender or food processor for a thicker syrup, but it will have the strawberry seeds, raspberry seeds or whichever in it..

Push through a sieve for a thinner syrup that has no seeds.

You can do this with most kinds of soft fruit, so use whatever's in season where you are. Berries are excellent, peaches work too. I haven't tried plums. If you want apples, just use applesauce. You could simmer down peeled and cored pears if you want, but it would end up more like pear sauce than syrup. Melons don't work well; just put balls or cubes of the melon on your pancake if you want to try that.

Bread Pudding

This can also be a dessert, depending on how you prepare it and what meal it is. But when I make it, I usually use it for breakfast, so it's in this section. It's a great way to use up stale bread. Not overly moldy – that changes the flavor, but bread – homemade and bakery bread that doesn't have preservatives especially – gets kind of dry and tough after a few days. This uses that up in a moist and delicious way.

You don't have to use old bread though; you can cut up any good bread, just let it sit out in a bowl to dry a little bit for a few hours before using.

This is a popular food worldwide, and many places have their own regional variations including everything from coconut milk to rum. This is the one I use (with a few variations following); you'll find many more if you look around. The recipe has a lot of leeway; you can use more eggs, or more milk, or less bread, or more fruit, and so on.

You can make this either sweet or savory. Read the recipe carefully; it is in sections. The first part is the same between them, and the second part makes the differentiation.

Half a loaf of stale bread (about 6 cups), cubed or broken into small pieces.

3 eggs, beaten

2 cups milk

3 T butter

For Sweet:

1/2 to 1 cup small cut fruit (raisins, chopped apples, cranberries, blueberries, etc.) if desired.

1/2 cup sugar

1 tsp cinnamon and/or nutmeg (can use allspice)

1 tsp vanilla

For Savory:

1 small/med onion

2 T oil

1 cup cheese

1 cup vegetarian meat substitute (optional)

1 cup vegetable of choice. (if a hard vegetable like cauliflower or carrots, zap in microwave to cook partially first.)

1-2 tsp seasonings – try an *herbs de Provence* blend, Italian blend, or rosemary, parsley, and oregano.

Grease a baking dish; I prefer using one of my large casserole dishes that has a lid.

Heat butter and milk in a pan until milk is warm and butter is melted. Try not to boil it. Cool it for a few minutes before adding to the beaten eggs. Cooling is important; hot milk will cook the eggs instead of mixing with them.

If savory: sauté onion in oil until golden brown.

Mix eggs and seasonings together. Add milk and mix well.

Toss bread and egg mixture in a bowl. Add fruit. (Or veggies and half the cheese. Save the other half to sprinkle on the top when it's put into the baking dish.)

Put into casserole dish, cover, and chill for at least an hour. You can prepare the night ahead of time and chill till morning, if desired.

When you're ready to cook it, first preheat oven to 325.

Cook for 55-65 minutes, until it's done. It will be mostly firm and knife inserted into center will come out clean. Remove lid for last 20 minutes of cooking.

Variations:

You can use half and half or heavy cream instead of milk. You can use coconut milk instead of milk.

You can use more eggs for a more solid, 'eggy' dish.

I encourage you to experiment with seasonings and mix-ins. This dish is great for using small bits of leftovers, or the bits of fruit or vegetables left after making other dishes. Try adding lemon zest and bit of lemon juice instead of the cinnamon, with blueberries or cranberries for a lemon-cranberry bread pudding. Try Italian spiced with cheese and vegan meatballs; cottage cheese and mandarin oranges; leftover cabbage, fake ham, and Swiss cheese.

Quiche

A quiche is a custard pie with almost anything you want in it. There are some things that just go together well; I'll give my favorites, but feel free to use whatever you've got. The fillings you use need to be cooked first and then cooled to room temperature, unless it's something really fast-cooking like spinach, herbs, or cheese, so it's a great way to use leftovers. I make a lot of them in the summer, because that's when my chickens are laying and my garden is putting out all kinds of delicious things.

1 blind-baked pie crust

The ratio for the custard is 1 egg per 1/2 cup of milk

4 eggs

2 cups milk

or if you have a lot of fillings or a small pie plate,

3 eggs

1 ½ cups milk

salt and pepper to taste

Whatever you've got to add to the quiche.

Preheat oven to 350.

Beat the eggs, then whisk in the milk. Mix in the fillings, and pour mixture into crust.

Bake at until set. (A knife inserted in the center will come out clean.)

Remove from oven and let sit 10 minutes before you cut it into slices.

Some good fillings for quiches are:

1 cup spinach, 1/2 cup feta, 1 crushed clove garlic, and 1 T fresh/1 1/2 tsp dried basil

1 cup chopped broccoli, 1/2 cup cheddar (or more, if you love cheese)

Chopped tarragon, parsley, and mozzarella

Vegetarian ham substitute and shredded Swiss cheese, with chives

Potato (cook first, or use leftover baked potatoes, cubed), sautéed onion, rosemary, chives

Cauliflower (again, remember to cook and cool it first, or used leftovers), cheese, nutmeg, chives

Frittata

Frittatas are similar to quiches, but not exactly a quiche without a crust. They are more of baked omelet. They have a lot less milk and more eggs, and they need to be cooked in a cast iron skillet or an oven-safe frying pan. You cook them by putting your egg and filling mixture in the greased pan on top of the stove and cooking there until the bottom and sides start to cook, then putting in the oven to finish off. Adjust the amount of eggs by the size of you pan; here's an average amount for a large-ish skillet.

8-12 eggs

1/3-1/2 cup milk, cream, sour cream, or yogurt. Don't use skim or low fat; better to skip dairy entirely than to use watery dairy.
Salt and pepper to taste (about half a teaspoon works well)

2-3 cups of add-ins, vegetables need to be pre-cooked.
About 2/3-1 cup of cheese, optional
Oil enough to grease the pan thoroughly (a bit more if you have to sauté your vegetables first)

Preheat oven to 375. (You can experiment with different heats to see which results you like better.)

You can precook the vegetables by sautéing them in the frying pan you are using, if they aren't already cooked. If they are, sauté them in the pan just enough to heat them up.

Beat the eggs, dairy, and salt and pepper until they are just blended; over-beating makes it puff up in a very non-frittata way. Mix in the cheese (You can keep half out to put on the top if you'd rather.)

Pour egg mixture over the vegetables, stirring briefly to ensure complete covering and even spread. If you are topping with cheese, sprinkle it over the top now.

Cook on stove top over low heat without stirring anymore just until the edges start to pull away from the pan slightly, around 5 minutes; immediately move to the oven.

Bake until set, about 15 minutes. It will not be runny at all, but will shake just a little bit when you gently shake the pan. Overcooked eggs don't taste great, and the pan is hot and will keep cooking for a few minutes after you remove it from the oven.

Let cool about 10 minutes, then cut and serve. Keep leftovers refrigerated.

You can freeze any that you don't think you'll eat right away; thaw in the refrigerator before reheating.

Oatmeal

Oatmeal is a really good breakfast that's easy to make and very inexpensive. There are different kinds of oats available, and they are cooked in different ways

-With Rolled Oats

Use a 3 parts water, 2 parts rolled oats (not instant), pinch of salt ratio.

Bring water and salt to boil, lower heat to a simmer, and add the oats. Mix them in.

Cook for 5 minutes uncovered, then cover and remove from the heat. Let sit for a few minutes and serve.

-with Steel-Cut Oats

This makes a chewier, more textured oatmeal that I think stays with you longer.

Use a 3 parts water, 1 part steel-cut oats, pinch of salt ratio. (You can use 4 to 1 for a smoother, porridge-like oatmeal; I like firmer.)

Bring water and salt to a boil. Add oats, bring to a rolling boil, then lower heat to low and keep at very low simmer.

Simmer for 20-30 minutes, stirring occasionally; check consistency at 20 minutes.

Serve with whatever toppings you like.

Get creative with toppings; if I'm making this for multiple people, I'll make an oatmeal bar with small bowls of brown sugar, butter, raisins, dried cranberries, fresh fruit, cream, coconut, chocolate chips, peanut butter, maple syrup so that each can doctor up their bowl as they want. I've seen people go savory and put in vegetables, cheese, herbs, avocados. Use what you have on hand. It's healthy (unless you go the chocolate chip route), and tastes great, especially on chilly mornings.

Rice and Raisins

This is one of my Grandpa B's favorite breakfasts – this and oatmeal and raisins. It's a good way to use of leftover rice.

1 cup cooked rice

1/4 cup raisins

Evaporated milk

Spoonful of brown sugar

Put the rice in a pan. Add the raisins. Pour in evaporated milk while mixing them together; add enough to make it kind of soupy.

Cook together on stove until well heated, put in a big spoonful of brown sugar and mix it around. Eat (straight from the pan, if you were grandpa.)

You can use different fruit, if you prefer.

Cornmeal Mush

This is a dish you can eat at either of two stages – the hot cereal phase, or the sliced loaf phase. Note the recipe is just 2 parts water to 1 part cornmeal, with a little salt. You can use those proportions to make however much you like.

1 ¼ cups cornmeal

2 ½ cups water

1/2 tsp salt

Combine all ingredients in a sauce pan and cook over medium heat, stirring constantly, until mixture thickens.

If you want to use it as a hot cereal, stop here. Put into bowls and serve with whatever hot cereal toppings and mix-ins you want.

If you want it in solid form, press into a loaf pan and chill completely. It will get stiff.

Remove from the loaf pan and cut into slices. Fry them in a small amount of oil, and serve with whatever sauce you want.

For breakfast, this is good with maple syrups, butter, fruit syrups, or brown sugar, or cinnamon sugar.

But it doesn't have to be for breakfast; you can serve it with vegetables and gravy for dinner, or as a side dish at one of the other meals.

French Toast

There are a lot of recipes out there, and some are pretty persnickety, but this is what I do. It's easy, it's delicious, and it's cheap.

Sliced bread – I prefer multigrain, because it's got flavor and texture, but whatever you have is good. It great with slightly stale or dry homemade bread.

For egg dip, use these proportions – I usually go 3-4 eggs and a cup of milk:

1 egg

1/3 cup milk

Flavorings, if desired

Beat the egg, flavorings, and milk together and put in shallow pan or bowl wide enough to use to dip bread.

Heat a frying pan over low-medium heat and grease lightly. Don't make it too hot – you want the bread to cook through. Too high a temperature will burn the outside and leave the inside mushy.

Lay a slice of bread in the egg mixture until one side is completely covered. Turn it over and get the other side.

Cook in frying pan slow enough that inside is done. Repeat until bread and eggs are used up.

If you've got left over eggs, you can just cook them up as scrambled eggs; cook slowly so the extra moisture from the milk cooks off or runs out.

Eat with butter and syrup, or brown sugar, or cinnamon sugar, or fruit – whatever you like.

I've seen people mix this up with orange juice instead of milk.

I usually add a pinch of cinnamon and few drops of vanilla – it tastes divine. You can try nutmeg or other flavorings as desired.

Egg-in-Bread

This is a different kind of bread and egg. Have enough butter in the pan to fry-toast the bread too, and it's pretty tasty.

1 slice bread – preferably a thick and large slice, with a firm crust.

1 egg

Butter

Salt and pepper to taste

Heat a frying pan over low-medium heat, and grease it. Butter or margarine is best for this – it will burn if you're not careful, but it goes well with this recipe.

Tear a circle 2-3 inches around out of the center of your slice of bread and lay it in the greased pan. Put the removed bread aside to use in one of the stale bread recipes (freeze till you have enough)

Crack your egg and put the egg in the circle you've made in the bread. Add a little salt and pepper on the egg, if you are using it.

Cook until egg is desired solidity, turning it over midway.

Good with a bit of cheese on top – after you've flipped the egg and bread, lay a slice of cheese on it to melt while the egg finishes cooking.

Granola

This is another recipe that is more of a formula. Keep an eye on the proportions, and you can swap in alternative ingredients in the same category. Making your own granola is far cheaper than buying it, and will probably be a lot healthier – store bought granola has a LOT of sugar in it, more than some of the frosted sugar bomb-type cereals. There is a lot of flexibility, so you can adjust your batch to match what you already have or what is most affordable this week.

4 cups rolled oats – not quick oats or steel cut oats. Can include other rolled grains like barley or buckwheat if you want, but oats are easiest to find and cheapest.
Spices totaling 1-4 tsp, depending how strongly you want it spiced (cinnamon, nutmeg, cardamom, allspice, ginger, etc.)
1 cup raw nuts and seeds, any combination (sunflower, flax, pumpkin seed; pecans, walnuts, pistachios; wheat germ, sesame seeds, etc.)
1/4 tsp salt

1 cup shredded coconut (optional, but I like it; can use sweetened or unsweetened)

1 ½ tsp flavoring (vanilla, almond, maple – your choice)

1/2 cup oil (butter, coconut, canola, etc.)

1/2 cup sweetener (honey, brown sugar, maple syrup, agave nectar...)

1/2 to 2 cups sweet mix-ins (dried fruit, chocolate chips)

Preheat oven to 300 and get out large baking dishes or cookie sheets.

Mix wet ingredients in small bowl or pan (if you're using brown sugar or solid fat like butter or coconut milk, you'll need to melt them to be liquid before they'll mix right.) This includes the vanilla or other flavoring extract.

Combine dry ingredients in a large bowl, excluding the fruit but including the spices. (Do not bake the fruit with the rest; it will burn.)

Add wet ingredients to dry ingredients and mix thoroughly.

Spread on baking sheet (use two if you need the room) and bake until golden brown, stirring every 15 minutes; this should take about 45 minutes to an hour.

It will not be completely dry when you take it out; it will finish drying as it cools. Once cool, mix finished granola with whatever fruit or sweet mix-ins you are adding.

Store in tightly sealed container.

Note the proportions of the ingredients to be baked – 6 parts dry to 1 part wet/sweet. In our example: 4 cups oats, 1 cup coconut, 1 cup nuts = 6. 1/2 cup oil, 1/2 cup sweet = 1 cup.

You can fiddle with this a little – I've seen recipes that use less oil and substitute in apple juice instead, or that use only 1/3 cup of each, and others that count the fruit as part of the 6 to 1 (I've not found that necessary, as fruit is not baked with the rest, so isn't part of this proportion.) But with 6 to 1 in your head, you are free to experiment with combinations of grains, nuts, and other add ins as you like.

There is wiggle room in the spices – I've seen recipes with as little as 1/2 tsp of cinnamon only, and others that want up to 4 tsp of combined spices. Start with 1-2 tsp combined; you can add more in your next batch if you want.

Baked Apple Pancake

My mom made this a lot when we were little; it's tasty, doesn't cost much, is filling, and gives you energy for the day.

4 cups apples, peeled, cored, and sliced

1/3 cup granulated sugar

2 tsp cinnamon

1 batch pancake batter, as described in an earlier recipe

1 ½ cups peanut butter

2/3 stick butter, softened

1/4 cup maple syrup, honey or pancake syrup(optional) You could use sugar but it makes the topping feel grainy

Preheat oven to 350 and grease a 9×13 inch pan.

Mix together the sugar and cinnamon. Toss the apples in the cinnamon sugar, and spread them in the greased pan.

Pour the pancake batter over the apples, ensuring they are completely covered.

Bake for half an hour, until toothpick inserted in center comes out clean.

While it bakes, beat together the peanut butter, butter, and sugar (if you're using it).

Spread peanut butter topping over the still-hot baked pancake.

Serve hot.

Sauces, Gravies, Dips

Food that goes over other food. That basically describes this chapter, and it sounds so simple, but a well-made sauce or gravy will set your meal or dish off just right.

This may be the most widely varied section. Think about it: the gravies that go over your biscuits, the marinara that coats your spaghetti, the caramel that goes over your ice cream, and salsa into which you dip tortilla chips all fall into this category.

So read on, cook on, and learn to set off your pasta, your biscuits, your potato dishes, and your ice cream. It's all in this chapter!

Grandma's White Sauce

This is a good base for a lot of things, depending on what you add into it. It's faster than the more traditional roux-based sauce – which I give a recipe for later. I think it has a less rich flavor, but it's also harder to scorch.

1/2 stick butter

1 T corn starch

1 cup milk

Melt butter in saucepan. Add corn starch and mix well

Mix in milk slowly, stirring continuously.

You might add cheese for a cheese sauce, veggie sausage for gravy, a pinch of onion powder, or just black pepper, depending on what you have available and the purpose for which you a making it.

Great-Grandma's Egg Gravy

Boil up eggs, a dozen or so, and use some for breakfast one day, and let the remaining three eggs get cold in the fridge.

The next day, make up a basic white sauce.

Peel the eggs, slice them, and gently add them to the hot gravy, stirring gently.

Add more salt and pepper when you add the eggs.

Serve over biscuits or bread.

Roux-Based White Sauce Base – the classic base you'll see in all kinds of sauces

2 T flour

2 T butter

1 cup milk

Melt the butter, mix with flour, and brown to make a roux.

Add the milk slowly, stirring the entire time.

Simmer until thickened

Continue with whatever you want to add. This is a base – while you can eat it plain, it's most often used with added seasonings, proteins, vegetables, or herbs. You'll see it turn up in a lot of sauce recipes; see the cheese sauce and country gravy for examples. Sometimes water is added instead of milk; see the Brown Gravy recipe for that.

Brown Gravy

This one is great with mashed potatoes, with cottage cheese loaf, or over roast or fried potatoes to make a kind of poutine. It's my husband's favorite, and he often asks if I'm making it.

2 T butter

2 T flour

1-1 ½ cups water

1-2 T vegetarian beef-like seasoning, such as McKay's

1/3-1/2 cup sour cream

1/2 T dried parsley

Make a roux from the butter and flour by melting the butter in your saucepan, then adding flour and stirring until it turns golden brown (or a bit darker if you like; that makes a richer flavor, but you have to watch carefully to avoid burning.)

While whisking constantly, slowly mix in 1 cup of water and stir until it thickens. If it looks thicker than you like, add a bit more water until it's the consistency you prefer. Don't add extra water too fast; it takes a few minutes before the gravy's thickened up, and too much water ends up with runny gravy.

Mix in seasoning mix; I left a range so you could adjust how strongly flavored you want the gravy. Remove from heat and mix in sour cream. Mix in parsley. Serve.

I've tried this with the chicken flavored seasoning, but the sour cream overwhelmed the flavor. If you left that out, you could use this to make chicken gravy.

Country Gravy

4 T butter

4 T flour

1-2 tsp black pepper

1 tsp salt

2 cups milk

Melt the butter in a saucepan or cast iron skillet. Whisk in the flour and heat until it turns a dark golden brown, stirring constantly.

Add salt and pepper.

Slowly whisk in the milk, stirring constantly to ensure no lumps and complete blending. Continue stirring until it gets thick.

Remove from heat and serve with biscuits.

You can add crumbled vegetarian sausage to this for sausage gravy. You can increase or decrease the black pepper to taste. You can try adding a pinch of garlic powder if you want, or sautéed onions. Both can taste good, but are not part of the classic country gravy preparation.

Mom's Vegetarian Vegetable Gravy – 2 Kinds

First Vegetable Gravy

This is what she used to serve at Thanksgiving until I learned to make the brown gravy and took over gravy making detail..

2 stalks of celery chopped fine

1 medium onion chopped fine

1 clove of garlic crushed

1/2 cup mushrooms diced to infinity so Fawn doesn't know they're there (that would be me)

2 T butter

1 can frichik, chopped small, plus the juice (Use whatever kind of vegetarian chicken substitute you got, except breaded; if it's not in a can, add 1/2 cup vegetable or chicken like stock)
1 can mushroom soup,

1 can water

Salt and pepper to taste

sauté the vegetables in the butter until soft.

Add the non-chicken, soup and water. (It can help to mix the soup and water together in a bowl before adding) and mix well.

Add salt and pepper to taste

Simmer until thickened and hot through.

Second Vegetable Gravy:

1 large onion, chopped

1/2 each of green, yellow and red peppers, chopped

2 lg cloves of garlic, smashed

1/2 cup vegetable broth
1 T butter.
1 cup of vegetarian beef substitute (Morningstar Grillers, reconstituted TVP, fresh seitan etc.)
1 can of mushroom or celery soup,
1 can of water or milk

Salt and pepper to taste

Melt the butter and add the vegetable broth. sauté the onion, peppers, and garlic in this until tender.

Add the can of soup and can of milk. Mix well. Add salt and pepper.

Continue to stir until heated completely.

Mom's Easy Mushroom Gravy

Mushrooms are one food I've never been able to warm up to (I usually substitute in cream of celery), but the rest of my extended family likes this a lot.

1 can mushroom soup

1 can milk

1 package vegetarian beef substitute, crumbled or chopped

1 T butter
1 tsp beef-like bouillon

Salt and pepper to taste

Brown the non-beef in the butter.

Add the soup, milk, and bouillon. Mix until thoroughly blended and warm through. Salt and pepper to taste.

She usually serves it with biscuits or hot rolls.

Grandma's Emergency, Low Supplies Gravy

1/2 cup white flour

2 cups water

Salt and Pepper

In a clean, dry pan, heat the flour over medium heat, stirring continually, until it's brown in color but not burnt.

Slowly whisk in the water.

Simmer and stir until thick. Add salt and pepper to taste.

You can use this as a base – add herbs, add chopped boiled eggs, add whatever you have to hand that might taste good. Try adding some well-matched herbs from the garden.

Cheese Sauce

2 T butter

2 T unbleached flour

1/4 tsp dry mustard powder

1 cup milk

1 1/2 cups sharp cheddar cheese, grated

Salt and pepper to taste

Make a roux by melting the butter over medium-low heat, then whisking in the flour and mustard powder and continuing to whisk until a light golden brown.

Whisk in the milk gradually, no more than a quarter cup at a time, stirring continually to be sure that roux and milk mix completely without lumps. (You can usually stir out any lumps that happen). Stir over med-low heat until sauce thickens.

Add the cheese, stirring until completely melted. Add salt and pepper as desired. Remove from heat.

This is good over a variety of veggies – it's included with a broccoli recipe back in that chapter. It's good over baked potatoes. It makes good homemade macaroni cheese when put over pasta. It makes a good base for a potato broccoli soup – add another cup or two of milk for a more soupy texture.

White Cheese Sauce

2 T butter

2 T unbleached flour

1 cup milk

1 package cream cheese

1/2-1 cup Parmesan, Romano, or blend of the two

Make a roux by melting the butter over medium-low heat, then whisking in the flour and continuing to whisk until a light golden brown.

Whisk in the milk gradually, no more than a quarter cup at a time, stirring continually to be sure that roux and milk mix completely without lumps. (You can usually stir out any lumps that happen). Stir over med-low heat until sauce thickens.

Cut the cream cheese up into chunks and add, stirring until completely melted.

Add the Parmesan cheese, stirring until completely melted. Add salt and pepper as desired. Remove from heat.

Now, there are a few ways to spice this, depending on what your end goal is. Try adding a couple cloves of garlic – just adding garlic adds a sharp garlic taste, sautéing garlic in a little oil or butter first adds a mellow garlic taste. Add basil, parsley, oregano, or Italian blend for an almost-Alfredo taste. (Alfredo uses heavy cream and butter instead of a white sauce base.) Rosemary, chives, or tarragon also all can be good. Try with *herbs de Provence.*

Marinara Sauce

There are bazillion ways to vary this one and personalize it. Here's a good start to your sauce explorations.

1 large can crushed tomatoes, or stewed tomatoes, run through a blender OR 4 cups fresh tomatoes, blanched, peeled, and chopped
1 onion, chopped

2 cloves garlic, crushed
4 T olive oil

1 tsp salt, if you are not using canned tomatoes – they already have salt

1 T fresh basil, chopped OR 2 tsp dried basil

1 T fresh parsley OR 2 tsp dried parsley

1 tsp fresh oregano OR 1/2 tsp dried oregano

1/4 tsp black pepper

2 T tomato paste
1 bay leaf, optional

In large pan, sauté the onion and garlic in the olive oil until light gold.

Add all other ingredients except tomato paste, bring to a boil, lower heat to a simmer, and partially cover (leave lid open a crack).

Cook for half an hour, adding tomato paste in the last ten minutes.

Toss with or pour over pasta and serve with grated Parmesan or Romano. Or just grated cheese. I think it's really tasty with little fresh mozzarella balls, if I can find them on sale.

There are a lot of ways to switch this up. You can simmer on a low heat for longer, skipping the tomato paste.

Try skipping either basil or oregano and using only one or the other. Increase the amounts if you want; I like a lot of basil and garlic, so I'll often double them when cooking for myself and my husband, who's gotten used to my cooking and claims to like it. A sprig of rosemary can make a nice addition, or some chili pepper for spice.

You can add other vegetables; try slivered or grated carrots, finely chopped celery, chopped spinach, artichoke hearts, diced green peppers, or chopped olives during cooking. Near the end of cooking, you can toss in asparagus spears, larger chunks of carrot, sliced or chopped summer squash, or broccoli.

Butter and Herbs on Pasta

This isn't so much a sauce, but a formula for serving with pasta. Its good for using if you haven't much else – pasta, butter, whatever dried herbs you've got. It's great in the summer if you have an herb bed or windowbox, or if you have herbs as houseplants. Fresh herbs, butter, and pasta just taste great together.

2 cups pasta

2 T butter

Chopped or dried herbs

Salt and pepper to taste.

Cook the pasta to al dente. Drain and return to pan.

Toss butter with pasta until it melts.

Toss in herbs, salt, and pepper until well mixed. Serve.

Good herbs for this are: chopped basil and garlic; tarragon; chives; rosemary; oregano; thyme; sage. Almost any savory herb, really; but not all together at once

Hollandaise Sauce

I love this sauce. It can be a bit tricky to balance melting the butter and NOT scrambling the eggs (totally ruins the sauce; you just have eggs swimming in butter then), but it's so worth it. It's good on eggs on toast or English muffins, it's great over vegetables (try with asparagus). It's just delicious. Note that it is a really high-fat recipe, with lots of butter, and plan the rest of the meal accordingly.

4 egg yolks

4 T Butter (has to be actual butter for this recipe)

1 1/2 to 2 T Lemon Juice

Cayenne or Paprika, optional

The object of mixing is to thoroughly mix the butter and eggs, without curdling the eggs. There are different techniques you can use to do this; try this one. You'll need a double boiler and whisk, or a pan of boiling water and a metal bowl that can fit over it without touching the water – it's very important that it not touch the water.

In the metal bowl, whisk the eggs and lemon juice together briskly. Continue whisking until doubled in volume and lightened in color.

Move to over the hot water, and beat continually. Add butter, 1 T at a time, whisking briskly until it melts. Move over and off of hot water as needed to slowly, slowly melt butter without scrambling the eggs. Continue until all butter is melded into the sauce. Add a dash of cayenne, if desired. Remove from heat and use immediately.

You can also try melting the butter without browning it and letting it cool. Then beat the eggs and lemon juice over the hot water; once they are light, heated, and doubled in volume, drizzle the cooled butter in, a little bit at time, whisking continually and removing from over simmering water as needed to avoid scrambling them; continue until all butter is melded in to the mixture, Add a dash of cayenne if desired, remove from heat, and use immediately.

You can increase the butter in this recipe, up to 2 T butter per egg yolk instead of 1, if you want. 1 to 1 is enough. You can make less at a time as well.

Hollandaise sauce does not reheat well. You can try slowly warming it over hot water, whisking continually, but it will usually separate into little bits of scrambled eggs in a pool of butter. Only make what you'll use at the meal, and use immediately.

Spinach Artichoke Dip

This is delicious, and you can make a huge batch for less than the cost of a single serving in a restaurant.

1 small onion, chopped

2-3 cloves garlic, crushed

2 T oil

1 bag frozen chopped spinach, thawed and drained (or 1 bag fresh spinach, washed and chopped)

1 can artichoke hearts, drained and coarsely chopped

1 package cream cheese, softened
1/2 cup mayonnaise, sour cream, or half and half of each
1 cup mozzarella, keeping 1/4 cup out for putting on top.
1/2 cup Parmesan

1/2 tsp salt

1/2 tsp black pepper

1 tsp oregano, optional

Preheat oven to 350 and grease an 8×8 inch baking dish, a pie pan, or a cast iron skillet.

Sauté the onions. After they start turning translucent, add the garlic and sauté for a couple more minutes. (You can skip this if you like sharper onion flavor; sautéing mellows the onion.)

Mix everything together thoroughly, except the 1/4 cup mozzarella for topping. If using fresh spinach, wilt it over heat before trying to mix it in.

Scrape it into the baking dish and spread it evenly, topping with the reserved cheese.

Bake for 25-35 minutes, until bubbling and golden brown around the edges. If it looks hot through and melty, but isn't as browned as you'd like, pop it under the broiler for 3 minutes or so.

Serve with tortilla chips, small chunks of bread, or pita chips.

You can also combine everything and put it in a slow cooker for a couple hours.

You can add a dash of chili pepper if you want some zing.

Bean Dip

2 cups cooked beans and 1 T oil OR 1 can refried beans

1/2-1 cup salsa – bought or homemade

1 cup shredded cheddar or Monterey jack cheese + 1/4 cup for topping

1/2-1 cup sour cream

2 cloves garlic, crushed

Preheat oven to 350 and grease a baking dish; OR get out a medium saucepan.

If using whole beans, run them through a blender with the oil; add a little (be cautious) water if they are too thick.

Mix everything except the 1/4 cup topping cheese together well, then either scrape into baking dish and top with held back cheese, and bake for 25 minutes, until hot and bubbly OR scrape everything into the saucepan and heat over med-low heat, stirring continually, until hot.

Serve with tortilla chips.

Salsa

There are a lot of possible salsa recipes; feel free to tinker with this till you find your favorite arrangement.

3 cups finely chopped fresh or canned tomatoes
1 onion, diced

3 cloves garlic, chopped

1-2 chopped bell peppers

1-2 chopped jalapenos, including seeds (don't include for milder salsa)

1/2 -1 tsp cumin

2 T lime juice

1/4 cup fresh minced cilantro (skip if you don't like cilantro)

1 cup corn (optional, added at end if you're using it)

Salt and black pepper to taste

Add chili peppers or use hotter peppers if you want spicy salsa

Combine everything and serve with tortilla chips, put on burritos, use in bean dips, etc.

If you want much less chunky salsa, or you want to skip all the hand-chopping, put everything in a food processor and blend it in 10-second bursts until it's all blended and the consistency you like.

7 Layer Bean Dip

1 can refried beans OR 2 cups beans, 1 clove garlic, and 1 T oil run through a blender together, then heated together (can be cooled after, just needs to be cooked)

1 tsp chili powder

1 tub sour cream

2 cups shredded lettuce

2 cups shredded cheese

1 diced tomato or 1/2 cup salsa

1 can black olives, sliced

Guacamole OR 1 can chopped chili peppers (whichever you like better)

Mix the beans and the chili powder, and spread that on your platter or in your pan for the 1st layer

Spread the guacamole or chilies over this layer

Spread the sour cream evenly for the 3rd layer

Cover the sour cream with the cheese.

Spread the lettuce over that.

Top the lettuce with the salsa, and the 7th layer is the olives.

Serve with tortilla chips or quartered soft tortillas.

If there are other toppings you want, you don't have to stop at 7 layers. You can add more. Or use fewer toppings if you don't like or use some of these; for instance, vegans would skip the cheese and sour cream.

Guacamole

There are a lot of recipes for this as well, some a simple as mash a ripe avocado with a few tablespoons of salsa. This is the one I make for myself when I'm in a guacamole mood; I usually eat the whole thing for dinner.

1-2 ripe avocados (unripe avocados will not smash well, and they don't taste as good; ripe ones will have a little give without being smooshy)

1 T lime juice (lemon in a pinch)

1 tsp or so dried cilantro
1/2 tsp dried garlic

Pinch or two of chili powder

Salt to taste

Get the flesh out of your avocado. (Cut it in half lengthwise, remove the pit, scoop flesh out with spoon.)

Put everything in a bowl and smash it with a fork until it's smooth and well blended. Taste test; add more of whatever seasoning you think it needs.

Eat with tortillas chips, or use to top burritos or 7 layer dip or haystacks.

Apple Sauce and Apple Butter (and other fruit butters)

These are amazing made fresh. They're not expensive, and not hard, especially if you have a slow cooker. You can make them in a regular cooking pot, but you have to spend more time stirring and checking to be sure they aren't sticking to the pot and burning.

Apple Sauce

12-16 apples, peeled, cored, and sliced, or enough to fill your pot 3/4 of the way

1/2 cup water (just enough to keep apples from sticking before they've cooked enough to let out juice)

Put the apples in your slow cooker or pot. Cover and cook on until soft, stirring occasionally. you'll need to stir more stove top than in slow cooker, which you can basically ignore between checking for softness.

As you stir and they they cook, apples will slowly fall apart and become sauce. Cook until they've reached the sauciness you want; I like a few apple pieces left.

You can add cinnamon if you want. I'll usually sprinkle it on when I eat it, instead of mixing it in.

A bowl of applesauce, with a spoonful of peanut butter, is a great snack.

A favorite breakfast of mine is peanut butter applesauce toast, which is just what it sounds like: toast, spread with peanut butter, with warm applesauce poured over it. It's delicious, cheap, and hearty. It's divine with homemade bread fresh from the oven....

Apple Butter (with notes for other fruit butters)

I only make this in a slow cooker, though, as with the apple sauce, you can do it stove top, but with a lot more stirring.

1 large pan of applesauce – say, a batch just like the one above. You can also start fresh with peeled, cored, sliced apples.

0-3 cups sugar, brown, white, or a combination. I go low, less than 1 cup, but it depends on your taste and how tart your apples are. Keep in mind sugar is a preservative; with lower sugar, you'll need to extra careful to keep refrigerated or frozen. You can use honey instead, if you have it available.

Spices to taste: 1-2 T cinnamon and pinch of salt to start, then add any of these (maybe not all; that's a bit much):

1/4 tsp cloves

1/2 tsp nutmeg

1/2 tsp ginger

1 T vanilla

1/4 tsp allspice

1 T lemon juice

I like ginger, lemon juice, and nutmeg, but you may prefer others.

Mix all ingredients together in slow cooker. If starting from apples, cook on low for 10-12 hours, covered the first 8 or so hours, then lid off to let extra water evaporate. If starting with apple sauce, cook with lid off until thickened and a rich brown in color. Use a blender to smooth out any remaining apple chunks.

For stove top, if starting from apples, cook, covered, for 1 hour, stirring occasionally, until soft. Then cook another hour, with the lid off, stirring occasionally, until thickened and a rich brown.

You can do this with other fruits, whatever you have available, and spices needed. Plum butter, peach butter, cherry butter, pear butter, and pumpkin butter are delicious.

Pumpkin Butter

You can use any cooked winter squash with this as well. The first step will be to prepare the pumpkin or squash (by cleaning it out, baking until soft, and running through a blender) or start with canned pumpkin.

4 cups pumpkin puree (1 large or 2 small cans. Puree, not pie filling.)

1/2 cup white sugar

1/2 cup brown sugar

3/4 cup apple juice or cider

2 tsp cinnamon

2 tsp dried ginger

1 tsp nutmeg

1/2 tsp cloves

2 T lemon juice

Combine all ingredients. If stove top, bring to a boil, lower to a simmer, and cook 20 -30 minutes, stirring frequently, until dark brown and thick. Keep refrigerated.

If in a slow cooker, cook, lid off, until dark brown and thick, stirring occasionally. Keep refrigerated.

Plum Butter

3-4 pounds plums, cleaned, quartered, and pits removed but skins left on.

1/3 cup water

1/2 cup brown sugar

1 tsp cinnamon

1/2 tsp cardamom or 1/4 tsp cloves

Put plums and water in slow cooker. Cook on high for a couple hours, stirring occasionally, until juices start to form.

The put lid on, lower heat to low, and leave all day or all night, checking sometimes to see how it's coming (unless it's nighttime, then just sleep and check in the morning). When the plums are soft, stir and add sugar and spices.

Run through a blender to get smooth. Eat.

For stove top, cook until plums are soft. You can add the sugar and spices immediately. Then blend, jar up, and eat. Can immediately, or freeze, if you're not going to be eating it all within a week or so. Keep refrigerated.

Adjust the spices as you prefer.

You're getting the idea – fruit, simmered over low heat for a long time until soft and dark (that's carmelization, and part of the amazing flavor), with some (optional) sugar and whatever spices match. Blend to get smooth, and there's your fruit butter. It's a great way to use fruit if you get a lot of it; say, you have a pear tree in your yard, or a relative does. You can freeze it in freezer bags or containers, or can it for later. It makes great gifts. And the fruit butter you make at home is much lower in sugar than what you find in the stores.

One additional idea for fruit butters: cover a cookie sheet with parchment paper, and spread it thickly with an even coating of fruit butter. Bake at 140 degrees (yes, that low) for 6 hours or so, until set up and no longer very sticky to the touch. Cut into strips while still on the paper, and roll the strips up – fruit roll ups! (You can go directly with fruit like strawberries or mangoes and skip the spicing/making butter step if you want – run through a blender with a spoonful of lemon juice and a couple spoons of sugar, spread on parchment paper, and bake).

Easy Chocolate Sauce

1 cup chocolate chips

1/2 cup heavy cream

Either put ingredients in top half of double boiler and melt, stirring occasionally, until completely smooth.

OR

Melt chocolate chips in microwave by putting in microwave-safe bowl and cooking at high, checking every 20 seconds and stirring, until heated through and smooth. Then add cream to bowl and stir until completely blended and smooth, heating in 10 second intervals if needed for mixability.

I tend to like less sweet chocolate sauces, so I'll cut the chocolate chips half and half with unsweetened bakers' chocolate, or simply use unsweetened chocolate and add sugar slowly until it's palatable.

You can add a tsp of vanilla, or 1/4 tsp of cinnamon, or 1/2 tsp of mint flavoring for different flavors of chocolate.

Homemade Caramel Sauce

1 cup granulated sugar

1/4 cup water

3/4 cup heavy cream

2 T butter

In a saucepan, combine the sugar and water. Use a saucepan bigger than you think you'll need, because when you add the cream it bubbles up a lot. Be sure the mixture is spread evenly across the bottom of the pan, then turn on medium heat. Do not leave unattended and don't stir yet. Watch as sugar melts gradually to a clear syrup, then as it darkens to a golden brown the color of honey.

Turn off the heat – remove from heat if it's an electric stove – and immediately add cream and butter. Now stir continuously as caramel bubbles up and subsides. Stir until it is completely blended and an even tan color.

You can serve immediately. Caramel can be stored for a few weeks in a refrigerated and tightly sealed jar. The cold will make it thicken up, warm carefully to serve by floating sealed jar in warm water.

If you want, you can add 1 tsp of vanilla (for a vanilla-y caramel), or up to 1 teaspoon of salt (for a salted caramel).

Butterscotch Sauce

Butterscotch is extremely similar to caramel, except it uses brown sugar, the salt and vanilla are not optional, and order of ingredient adding is different. It's surprising how much a difference in flavor this makes.

4 T unsalted butter

1/2 cup packed dark brown sugar

1/2 cup heavy cream

Pinch salt

1 tsp vanilla

Melt the butter in a saucepan over medium heat, then whisk in the brown sugar.

Now add the heavy cream, whisking it in thoroughly. Continue to stir and bring mixture to a light boil or simmer; do not bring to heavy boil and do not stop stirring, or it will stick and burn. Let simmer (lower heat if needed to keep it only at a simmer) for 5-7 minutes.

Remove from heat, whisking continually, and add salt and vanilla.

Let cool to room temperature and serve.

Put remainder into tightly sealed container and keep refrigerated up to 2 weeks.

Equipping your Kitchen

I love looking at kitchen gadgets. There are so many nifty, creative things to see and imagine using! When you check the kitchen supplies aisle in a department store, there are thousands of items. There are even more if you look in a shop focusing on kitchens only. It can be overwhelming (and tempting) to look at the shiny things and think about what you'd do with them. But you don't need all of those things. Some are essential, some are not necessary (but incredibly useful), some help a little bit, and some just take up kitchen space and you end up throwing or giving them away to get the space back. The category each falls into depends a lot on how and what you cook – I don't need or have a cherry pitter, but if I had a cherry tree and wanted to make pies with my fruit, I might then need and get one. With a little looking, you can usually find what you need at a thrift shop, yard sale, or clearance sale.

Utensils

Knives and other sharp things

You will need some decent knives. You'll use them for peeling, slicing, dicing, chopping, cutting finished food, and slicing pies and bread. There are a wide variety of knives available, but you don't need all of them. Basics knives you'll need include a small paring knife, a medium chopping knife, and a larger slicing knife. The paring knife is for peeling and making smaller cuts; it's the knife I find myself using the most often. The medium blade is the next, for slicing potatoes, chopping onions, and so on. I have a few of these; serrated, pointed, and larger for chopping. The large knife is for slicing bread or other large things; you need a blade long enough to reach across the whole loaf.

You might also want to get a knife sharpener. It's important to keep your blades sharp, because dull blades can be dangerous – you can push too hard to try to cut something, and the blade slips and gets you. There's also the simpler risk of squashing what you're trying to cut instead of slicing it – think of putting too much pressure on a tomato and the potential mess.

There are other sharp tools you'll want to acquire for your kitchen. A potato peeler is very useful; you can peel with your paring knife, but the peeler makes it much easier, faster, and less likely to waste food. Kitchen scissors are handy. You'll use them to cut parchment paper for lining baking dishes, cut up herbs, cut string, etc. If you make pizza, sheet pies, pasta from scratch, or other foods that need to be cut into strips, you'll want to add a pizza cutter to your arsenal of sharp things.

Measuring Cups

There are different sizes and shapes of measuring cups. Some are just that – cups with markings up the side indicating how much is up to the marking. Others are sets of graduated cups – 1 cup, 1/2 cup, 1/3 cup, 1/4 cup, 1/8 cup, then a set of spoons. I like to have at least two measuring cups, though right now I have more; that way when cooking, I can use one for dry ingredients and one for wet. What I do most often is use my marked cup for wet ingredients and the graduated set for dry. I prefer glass cups for wet ingredients, because oil is difficult to clean off of plastic.

Measuring Spoons

Measuring spoons usually come in sets of tablespoon, teaspoon, 1/2 teaspoon, 1/4 teaspoon, 1/8 teaspoon. I have the same in my measuring spoons as I do for measuring cups; one set for wet ingredients, like vanilla or oil, and another for dry, like cinnamon or baking powder. You can use the same set; in that case, try to plan out measuring the dry before the wet, or your dry ingredients will stick to the spoons. Measuring tools are readily available and can be pretty cheap; I see them often in thrift stores and dollar stores.

Can Opener

You'll need a can opener. There are a surprising variety of can openers available, from small (and harder to use) ones designed to pack small for camping or cookouts, to pricey ones that cut sideways (supposedly to decrease sharp edges), to electric ones. A basic handheld can opener will work. They can be found cheaply, although if you can, get one that's a little more mid-range – it'll stay sharp longer. I've had handles break right off of super cheap ones; having to replace them doesn't save money.

Serving Spoons

You'll want a few varieties of serving spoons. Slotted spoons, for draining unwanted fluid off before you move the food from the pan, and solid, for scooping up sauces, gravies, and soups without all the fluid running out. You might also want a ladle, for serving gravies and sauces that are not mixed in with the main ingredients. You might want to see about getting small and large of each, for serving different kinds of food – big spoon for mashed potatoes, ladle for gravy, smaller spoon for peas, and so forth.

Spatulas

You'll need spatulas. There are two main categories of utensils that are both called spatulas, and you'll want some of each. There are plastic or metal ones that are used to serve food and to cook; you'd use them for actions like stirring or flipping eggs as they cook, flipping pancakes, or serving casserole from a baking dish. And there are plastic or rubber ones that are used to stir food while you prepare it, and to scrape a mixing bowl cleanly into the cooking dish. You'll use both kinds constantly as you cook and serve food.

You may want a pie turner, which is a triangular spatula used for serving pies, round cakes, and other foods that cut into triangular shapes.

Wooden Utensils

Wooden spoons are useful for stirring and for serving. They tend to have less deep bowls than other spoons, and I find them preferable when mixing things together. You can also lay a wooden spoon across the top of a boiling pan, and it will prevent the pan from boiling over much – the boiling-up food liquid will hit the spoon and go no further. There are also wooden spatulas.

Whisk

There are several shapes of whisk, but a basic wire whisk that's shaped like a teardrop is sufficient. You'll use the whisk for beating eggs, sauces, hot chocolate – all kinds of smooth, liquid foods. You might be whisking (called beating) during preparation or during cooking, or both. You can beat with a fork, but a whisk makes it easier and faster, and produces a smoother result if you're making gravies or sauces.

Brush

Pastry brushes are used to brush butter, oil, eggs, or milk over the surface of dough or pasty. I use mine more than I'd thought I would, so you'll probably want one. When I don't have one, I find myself spreading things with a paper towel or my bare hands, and that's just messy.

Grater

A grater helps you cut and shred ingredients. You will use it to shred cheese, potatoes, carrots, zucchini – anything that needs to be in small bits. There are graters that stand up, and have different size shred on each of 4 sides; I've used these a lot over the years, and they work reasonably well. There are graters that are flat and have the different options at different spots on the plane; these are cheap, but I don't like using them at all; I keep getting on the wrong grate, or catching my fingers. Only get that if that's all that's available, or if you are packing for a camping trip or something and need to save space. There are graters that are basically the lid to a box, and the grated food goes into the box. These often have the option of changing out the grate surface, for small shreds, ordinary shreds, or slices. That's what I've got now, and I really like this option.

Kitchen Towels, Hotpads, Tea Towels, Aprons

You'll find yourself using these fabric items constantly. They're often available in thrift stores or on clearance, and aprons are easy to make. Towels are too, but the fabric's harder to come by cheaply.

Kitchen and tea towels are small towels you use in the kitchen. You'll use them to handle hot dishes, to wipe surfaces, to cover dough while it's rising, to wipe your hands one, to dry dishes with, and to place food on while it cools, or just to keep it off the countertop. Don't use the same cloth for cleaning and for food covering! Use a clean towel when in contact with food. Wash them frequently.

Aprons are also useful, especially if you are cooking or mixing something that tends to be messy. You can just pin a towel around yourself, but if you find or make an apron for a reasonable cost, you'll be using it often. It keeps your clothes clean while you cook; no matter how careful you are, flour puffs up, fluids splash, juicy tomatoes spit when sliced, and so on. You can use an apron to quickly dry your hands after washing (that or a kitchen towel). In a pinch, you can double or triple the fabric and use it to move a hot pan. It's also a universal sign of "I'm cooking", so could cut down interruptions while you're preparing food.

Hotpads are made of heat-resistant fabric and protect your hands when you need to handle hot pans. They can be any shape or formed as a glove. You can also use them to protect surfaces on which you are about to put a hot pan. They are not expensive and are useful, though you can use a folded kitchen towel to do many of the same things.

Dishes

Mixing Bowls

You'll want at least 3 mixing bowls – small, medium, and large. I find having a few sizes makes a difference. I have VERY large one for large batches of bread (5 or 6 loaves at a time) or large salads, and a few regular large ones for mixing up cookies, smaller batches of bread dough, casseroles, pasta and sauce, and so on. The medium and small ones are great for either smaller batches of food, or for those recipes that have you mix dry and wet ingredients separately and then blend them. I have a set of bowls that has a spout like a pitcher – small, medium, large. I find that feature useful for pouring out batter neatly into cupcake pans, popover pans, skillets for making pancakes, etc.

Baking Dishes

You'll want a several kinds of baking dishes. Loaf pans are used to make bread, some casseroles, cottage cheese loaf (it's like a vegetarian meatloaf), and so on. Cookie sheets are used for cookies (of course), pizza, roasting potatoes or other vegetables, and putting underneath pie pans so the pie doesn't overflow all over your oven. Pie pans are for pies, quiches, maybe rolls. Cupcake pans are good for cupcakes, rolls, little tarts, individual sized egg casseroles, and so on. You'll often find yourself using a couple of casserole dishes with lids, in whatever size suits your household.

Pots and Pans

You will need cooking pots as well. You'll want saucepans, a large cooking pot, and a skillet, with the requisite lids. I recommend a 4 quart pot, a 2 quart saucepan, a 1 quart saucepan, and at least a 10 inch skillet.

Electric Tools

There are several tools that make cooking a lot easier. There are even more that are only useful for a few things, and that can be easily passed over.

Electric Mixer

You'll use your electric mixer constantly. Get the best one you can afford; that might be whatever one is in the thrift shop, or it might be a fancy KitchenAid stand mixer. You'll use it for mixing dough, sauces, beating eggs, making icing, batter of all kinds, blending casseroles, and on and on. Good mixers can also handle heavy jobs like bread dough; some smaller or cheaper mixers may have some difficulty with that. I had a cheap hand mixer for years – I still have it, but when I got a decent stand mixer (refurbished and on sale, or else it would have been too expensive), I found the joys of letting the mixer do the kneading.

Food Processor

While you *can* make piecrust and biscuits by painstakingly rubbing the butter in with your hands, it's a lot faster to toss it in the food processor and hit pulse a few times. (Some stand mixers can also be used for this; check the specs on yours.) Likewise for grating multiple zucchini – you can do it by hand, tiring out your arm and chancing your fingers, or feed it into the processor and it's done in seconds. When making crumbs for crusts or stuffing, instead of rolling crackers or dried bread over and over with a rolling pin until it's suitably crumbled, whiz it in the processor, and on and on. Food processors are just plain useful; they speed up a lot of food preparation, and decrease the amount of effort it takes if it's a larger job.

They're nice but not necessary – you can to everything they do with hand tools, or even just a knife. But it's nice to be able to choose – hmm, just on carrot, I'll use a grater. A whole bag's worth – getting out the food processor. They're also not usually cheap, so keep your eyes open for a good-condition secondhand one or for a good sale. I got mine, new in the unopened box, at a yard sale.

Slow Cooker

These are also handy for a lot of things. They're not necessary, though; you can do anything you'd use it for with ordinary pots and pans, and faster. But if you've got a busy day, tossing food into the slow cooker and coming home to a ready meal is great. I use mine for making beans, applesauce, tomato paste, soups, and curries. You can use some varieties as small ovens, baking bread and potatoes.

Blender

This also falls under the category of really nice, but not necessary. You can make your own smoothies or blend soups and sauces so that they are perfectly smooth in a blender. I find myself only using mine occasionally, so consider what you like to make and choose accordingly. If you like smooth soups, you'll want one to run the finished soup through (one of the things I still use mine for). If you like iced drinks, make your own in a sturdy blender. You can use it to de-lump gravy that didn't come out quite right, or to make your own milkshakes. There are a couple kinds of blenders; the kind that is a pitcher with whirling blades at the bottom, and as an immersion tool, blades on a stem that you just lower into your bowl or pan.

Microwave

I think you already know about this one, but it's another useful kitchen gadget that's not absolutely necessary. I use mine daily, to reheat leftovers, thaw out frozen foods, quickly bake a potato, or to quick-steam vegetables.

Other Gadgets

Some of how you stock your kitchen has to do with your own habits and what you like most, as well as what resources you have for stocking up. I have several other kitchen gadgets I use sometimes, that are not necessary but that I use rather a lot. My toaster oven seems to cook roast veggies faster than the regular oven – though only in small batches. It's also great for making toasted sandwiches. I have a pizza cooker, which I may use a little more often than is healthy, but is still handy. It was a gift; I'd probably not bother buying one with a perfectly functional oven. I tend to use those both particularly when I don't want to heat up the whole oven; so mostly for small, quick baking of things (making one sub sandwich, or just two cookies), or in the summer when I'm trying to avoid heating up the house the way the large oven does. I use my electric kettle every day to heat water for coffee and tea; that's something that a stovetop kettle, or a quick zap in the microwave, could do just as well. I've got a waffle iron (only used sometimes, but was just a few dollars at Goodwill), and my husband has a sandwich maker (I don't like how it does sandwiches; he uses it constantly).

Paperware

There are various paper and plastic goods that you'll want to keep stocked in your kitchen; you'll use them while cooking and when putting things away. They are not absolutely necessary – people lived without them for ages – but they do make things easier.

Aluminum foil is familiar, and you probably already have some. It is used most often for covering baking dishes if they don't have lids, for covering food for storage and transport. Its stiffness helps provide the food with some protection and helps to keep it in place firmly once crimped down; you can be sure it is curved to avoid sticking to cheese on top, or frosting. Its disadvantages in comparison to plastic wrap are that it is not air tight, so food can get dried out. If you have bread or a food you don't want drying, you'll use plastic wrap.

Plastic wrap is a thin, plastic film. It sticks to itself and to smooth surfaces, allowing a seal that helps keep food from drying out, or helps keep 'refrigerator flavor' from getting into food that you are storing in the cooler. You can't use it on hot dishes or while cooking or baking, because it will melt all over your food and dishes.

Parchment Paper is not sensitive to heat, and is often used to line baking dishes when you are making cakes, cookies, or other sweets. It helps keep them from sticking to your pan; for cakes, that's especially important, as, even with greasing, the bottoms often stick and chunks break out of the cake. Parchment paper ensures the cake comes cleanly out of the pan. I cooked for decades without it, so it's not necessary, but now that I've started using it, I always use it when making a cake or pastry, and often use it with cookies.

Waxed paper is paper covered in a thin layer of food-safe wax. This makes it water resistant. It was used before the advent of plastic wrap, when people would use it, for instance, to wrap a sandwich well to keep it from drying out. It's used now for keeping food from sticking together. In general, parchment is for hot and waxed paper is for cold. You'd put waxed paper between layers of food you are trying to freeze. You'll find it between cheese slices in packages of sliced cheese. You might use it to line a pan in which you are making fudge, or no-bake refrigerator cookies.

Storage Supplies

Being able to store the food safely, so that it doesn't spoil and doesn't attract vermin is important. There are a LOT of ways to store your food. For completely free storage, you can just wash and reuse the glass jars that other food came in, or reuse the plastic containers from sour cream or cottage cheese. However, sometimes these are not good enough. Repurposed food containers don't work well for freezing food; glass jars break, and plastic containers may not seal well enough.

Storage Containers

Containers to put leftovers in the fridge can be had for free by reusing sour cream containers. On the other hand, that makes it hard to tell if you have sour cream or two week old leftover green beans. They are also too small for some purposes; you'll want a large, well-sealing bin for your flour, cornmeal, oatmeal, and sugar. And you will need to put them in a well-sealed container; in most kitchens, if you don't have foods securely sealed away, you'll get weevils, miller moths, ants, or worse pests. Reusing tightly-lidded jars can work for other foodstuffs, like chocolate chips, raisins, or crackers, if they don't come in packaging that will seal well. You can buy reusable plastic freezer boxes and jars for storing food for reasonable prices, and find larger, sealed containers for nonperishables, cereals, staples, and the like. Sometimes you can find good storage containers second-hand, as another way to keep costs down.

Storage Bags

The kind with the zippered top is best for keeping food sealed up securely. You can throw them away between uses, but these can also be washed and reused several times, to reduce waste and save money. You can use them to put away leftovers, and to protect food in cupboards; I'll often just put the box of crackers inside a gallon-sized zipped storage bag, and they don't get stale as fast and don't attract bugs, which are a real concern in my area of the country. Same for dry pasta, beans, and rice.

Freezer Bags

There is a difference between regular storage bags and freezer bags. Freezer bags use stronger zips and thicker plastic. Regular bags might get brittle and tear when exposed to freezing temperatures, and they won't protect your food as well. Freezer bags let you do just that – freeze food safely for weeks at a time. Use this for leftovers you won't be using soon, or to freeze produce that otherwise wouldn't be used before going bad.

Any food that's has an odor or is accessible can attract mice, rats, or insects, which is both unsanitary and wasteful (you should _not_ eat food that has insects or mouse droppings or signs of chewing), so be sure it's sealed up safely in storage containers or bags.

Stocking Your Pantry

Keeping basic supplies in your pantry makes it easier to plan meals, shop for supplies, and balance your diet. You *can* make a meal with as little as cornmeal and water, but planning and stocking your pantry will mean you have more choices than that.

You also have more control over what you eat. As we've talked about already, a lot of the really processed foods are not very good for you. Eating fewer processed foods, more home cooked, with whole ingredients, and keeping an eye on fat and sugar content, will help you be healthier, control your weight, and feel better. Just cooking on your own means there will likely be less processed sugar – even the dessert recipes here that have a cup or so of it are lower sugar than premade mixes that have it as the first, thus primary, ingredient. It also tastes better; since I've started baking and cooking more, I'm choosier about what I get eating out, or what quicker mixes I keep for occasions when time for cooking is especially short (and there are times; I'm not going to say stop everything, but cut back to only occasionally.) You'll find that after eating cakes baked with whole ingredients and without preservatives, a lot of store made cakes and mixes taste of chemicals instead of chocolate, or preservatives instead of butter and vanilla.

If you buy staples and shelf-stable items when they are on sale, you save money by stocking up when things are cheaper. The following chapter is my list of what to buy when it's available and keep on hand. This isn't meant to be a complete list of everything you keep – you'll have your own preferences, and stock accordingly. But if you have most of these thing readily available, you'll be able to whip up balanced meals in a trice. Most of these thing are inexpensive, readily available, and can keep for awhile (fresh produce and dairy excepted), so you'll be able to buy them when they're on sale, or when you find them in a bent and dent or discount store, and have them at hand when you need them.

Remember to keep food in tightly sealed containers or bags. In the pantry, it keeps them from getting vermin. In the fridge, it protects them 'refrigerator taste', and in the freezer, it slows getting freezer burnt.

Flours – *Wheat, White, Cornmeal, Other Grains* – You'll want to keep a store of flours, as they're an ingredient in many recipes. For white flour, get unbleached and enriched; white doesn't have as much nutrition, but enrichment at least lowers the deficit. White flour has a more delicate texture and is raises easier and lighter when leavening agents work on it, so it is needed for things like cakes that you want to be light. For many other foods, you'll make a blend of white and wheat, in the proportions you want. You can substitute up to half whole wheat flour in most recipes without compromising them. Whole grain flour is a little heavier and has more flavor to it than white. I prefer to use it in most things, except light dessert-type baked goods, because I like the flavor and texture. There is also a flour now called 'white whole wheat', which is a lighter whole flour, but not as light as plain white or cake flours. Cornmeal is used in a lot of recipes; get stone-ground if you can. There are other flours you can get and use: dried bean flours, other grains like barley or oat, rice flour, coconut flour, nut flours, and so on. These tend to be more expensive than wheat flours, but they are useful in other ways – some are lower carb if you're diabetic, or gluten free if you have celiac, or have different flavors or textures for particular recipes (say, an almond-flour tart crust). Buy them if you need and will use them. Check storage requirements; some specialty flours need to be refrigerated.

Oatmeal – Preferably not instant oatmeal. Get rolled oats and cut oats. Cut oats, I think, make the best hot cereal of the two; they are chewy and filling. And rolled oats, in addition to breakfast, are useful for baking. They can be added to bread or pancakes for added body, are used in many cookie recipes, are part of a lot of patty recipes, and can be used to make your own granola.

Baking Soda – also known as sodium bicarbonate. Many modern recipes use it in addition to powder. Older ones had just it. Baking soda is a base, as far as its PH, so if it's in a recipe, it will be conjunction with an acid like buttermilk or cream of tartar; the combination of the two makes a fizzing effect that makes things like buttermilk pancakes and buttermilk biscuits raise light and high. If you don't have the base of the soda balanced with the right amount of acid, it will taste odd. Baking soda is a lot stronger than baking powder; it takes only a third or a quarter to get the same effect.

Baking Powder – a recent innovation, as far as leavenings go. It is baking soda and cream of tartar already combined, so that the acid-base interaction is already balanced. Older recipes will still use cream of tartar and baking soda as separate ingredients. Baking powder is more forgiving when you're experimenting than baking soda, and is good for recipes that don't have an acidic component already. It's also a lot easier to get a light raise with this than the even older method of carefully folding in beaten egg whites.

Sugar – *Brown and White.* Both sugars have their uses. White sugar is highly processed; I've found that many recipes that call for it can have the amount cut by a quarter to a third without much effect. This won't work for really sensitive recipes, but I've used it often in quickbreads and cookies. White sugar has no flavor other than sweet. Brown sugar has a slight flavor – less for light brown, more for dark. I like the flavor, and will often use it in my coffee or tea, The brown color comes from a slight coating of molasses on the grains; it will dry out and stick together if not kept in a tightly sealed container. (If it dries out, seal it up with a slice of fresh bread overnight; that will moisten it.) It is often less processed than white sugar, though not always. There are two ways it is produced – one is to refine it less, leaving some of the natural molasses, and the other way is to add molasses to refined white sugar. Aim for the first kind, if you can. There are other sugars available, but they are costly – for instance, maple sugar tastes divine, but costs many times the price of ordinary sugar. Sugar is used in recipes for sweetness, flavor, and bulk; other sweeteners like stevia or artificial sugars don't caramelize or provide as much volume, and the baking will not turn out well.

Molasses – Molasses is a sweetener that has a strong flavor; unsulfured molasses is milder, and blackstrap molasses is very strong. It is the concentrated juice of a sugar cane; the more sugar that extracted from the syrup to make refined sugars, the stronger the flavor (and higher the nutritional content) of the remaining molasses. Some people like the flavor a lot – my dad will use it on toast. Others not so much; I'll use it in molasses cookies, gingerbread, and some pies, but won't spread it on *my* toast..

Salt – A vital and ubiquitous seasoning. You'll use it in most foods in small amounts; don't overdo it. Your body needs a certain amount of salt to function; without it, you'll die. Most processed foods severely overdo it, using salt instead of quality seasonings and ingredients, with the result that people overdose on salt and develop heart and kidney problems as the body tries to deal with the excess. A normal amount, as that in the recipes in this book, is healthy. We get used to the really strong salt flavor, so experiment with cutting back on it a bit to keep your intake healthy.

Oils – *vegetable, coconut, olive* – different oils serve different cooking purposes. Fats are necessary for your body in certain amounts, but easy to overdo. Our bodies tend to crave fats, even when we don't need them, both from conditioning and because bodies instinctively want this source of longer-lasting energy. Unless you're an athlete, you don't need a ton, and even then, choose wisely. Light vegetable oils have very little flavor, and are used for cooking things that you don't want that added flavor in. They also can handle higher temperatures than olive oil or coconut oil. Olive oil has a pleasant flavor in savory applications; it's not used as much with sweet dishes (though you certainly can). When making roasted veggies, it adds something to the flavor of the dish. It and coconut oil are good for medium-high temperatures. Coconut oil is solid at room temperature; it's useful when baking and can be used in a lot of recipes as a partial or complete substitute for butter (though that does change the flavor a bit). It is a very stable oil, and is great for cooking. Coconut oil can also be used in skin care. I use a little bit on hair after washing, and drop a couple tablespoons in a bath, especially in winter, to prevent drying of skin.

Butter or Margarine – Margarine is cheaper, but butter is less processed. There is some debate as to which is less bad for you. In my experience, butter tastes better and bakes better. But you can bake delicious things with sticks of margarine as well, if butter (at 3-5 times the price) is too costly, or you are trying to have more vegan food in your diet. In the recipes below, I'll use the word butter when I'm listing ingredient, but decent margarine will work in most. If for some reason margarine won't work for that recipe, I'll say so. Don't overdo either; too much straight fat, no matter what the source, is unhealthy. If using margarine, look for one that is 70% or so oil. *Don't* try to bake or cook with low fat margarine; it substitutes water or whey with gelatin for the fats, and will not bake well, just return to water and ruin your dish. It's only good for spreading on bread.

Seasonings – These have their own section further down, where they are talked about in more detail. Seasonings are what take food from bland to delicious; learning how to season your food well is a vital part of cooking.

Legumes – l*entils, dried beans, split peas, peanuts, tamarind, chickpeas, soybeans, and so on.* These are important sources of protein, fiber, and minerals in a vegetarian or vegan diet. They're used in all kinds of recipes and you should eat some most days. They are cheap, store well, and highly nutritious; I have in my pantry right now dried lima beans, kidney beans, two kinds of lentils, black beans, white beans, split peas, and pinto beans. And all of them together cost less than ten dollars. I've also got a couple cans of precooked beans – they are more expensive (1.19 for a bag of beans, or for a can of beans, and the bag has 12-15 servings, the can has 3.5), but they're useful if I'm in a hurry or didn't plan ahead enough to cook beans.

Rice – *Brown or white*. The difference is similar to that between whole wheat flour and white flour. Brown rice has only had the hull removed, and still has its bran and endosperm. It is significantly higher in nutrients, including fiber, iron, and B-vitamins. It is less tender and doesn't get sticky, meaning that for some recipes it won't work. White rice has had the bran and germ removed; it has less flavor and fewer nutrients, but a more pleasant texture for some foods. There are a wide variety of kinds of rice – jasmine, long grain, short grain, sticky – and each has a purpose. I usually just get medium grain, as I don't specialize enough for the others. Be aware that thanks to pollution from chemicals used in industrial farming before we knew how dangerous it was, brown rice sourced from certain areas (usually the US) may be higher in arsenic. It's not high enough to make you ill as long as it's part of a varied diet. Rinse rice before cooking, to be sure it's clean and to remove extra starches. I always boil rice in extra water and drain and rinse it, but that's not necessary and some methods of preparating rice, like making sticky rice, specifically forbid doing that or the stickiness won't happen.

Pasta – different shapes and sizes. I like to use whole grain pasta; it's more nutritious and tastes good. I buy it when it's on sale, because it is a little more than ordinary pasta. Keep a few shapes on hand; while you can make macaroni cheese with spaghetti noodles, somehow it just doesn't seem the same as when it's make with elbow macaroni or rotini noodles. Don't forget egg noodles; they're great with butter and herbs, or for baked cheese casseroles. You can make your own pasta, but it's a LOT more work and not a lot cheaper. My grandmother's basic noodle recipe is later in the book.

Canned vegetables – Stock up when they're on sale or when you find them in the bent and dent. Keeping canned foods stocked up is easier than frozen, as chances are you have a lot more shelf space than freezer space. Canned vegetables can just be kept in a cupboard, and I freeze enough from my garden and as meal prep that freezer space is at a premium, so I use canned for the things that are as good canned as frozen. Find out which veggies you think taste better canned or frozen. For instance, I don't like canned spinach at all, so I get it frozen for similar cost. Green beans and corn are fine canned, and canned tomatoes are cheaper than fresh and easier to find than frozen. Don't forget to get canned pumpkin when it's on sale around the holidays.

Coconut milk – Useful in a variety of recipes. I like to make a curried cauliflower soup that uses coconut milk; it's also a good liquid for making a tasty fruit soup.

Canned fruit – is usually less expensive than frozen. It's a toss up whether it costs less than fresh; usually what's in season is cheaper fresh. Canned pineapple is less than fresh most times, but tastes very different; be aware of what you like better. Read the labels and get fruit that is canned in juice instead of in heavy syrup, which is incredibly full of sugar. You can use the juice from canned fruit as a sweetener, or add it to smoothies or pitchers of other fruit juices. Keep a good store of different kinds when it's on sale, or stock up from orchards and can some of your own.

Pasta sauces – There are a lot of sauces you can make easily, but you might prefer to keep a few jars of whatever was on sale in your cupboard. Be sure to read ingredients to check for how much added sugar there is, and to check for odd chemical preservatives or unexpected meat products.

Fresh Vegetables and Fruit – Shop seasonally. Don't buy more than you'll use before it goes bad, or than you can prepare in other ways or preserve. I just made and froze a lot of banana bread because it was cheaper to get bananas in ten-pound cartons at the store I was at. Some things, like berries, only keep for a couple days; use them immediately. Don't buy berries unless you will use them right away, or you will freeze them; I've had several cartons of raspberries go grey and fuzzy because I thought, "oh, I'll eat them tomorrow". Other fruits, like apples and oranges, will be fine for a week or maybe even longer if kept appropriately (refrigerate citrus; keep apples cool). Some vegetables like cabbages, onions, and root vegetables, will keep for a several weeks at a time if you store them in a cool, dark place. Good produce to keep on hand are apples, cabbages, onions, lettuce, carrots, and bananas, as well as whatever's in season or what you need for planned recipes for the week.

Frozen Vegetables – Some vegetables keep best when they're frozen, rather than canned; examples are cauliflower and broccoli. I keep frozen cauliflower, broccoli, and spinach on hand; when I have room or it's a good sale, I'll keep green beans, peas, and carrots.

Frozen Fruit – If you want to and can afford to keep berries on hand, frozen is a good way to do it. Otherwise, I tend to use fresh or canned, as they are (at least in my geographic area) a bit less expensive.

Potatoes – As mentioned above, keep potatoes at hand. They're used in a lot of recipes, and they're good just on their own.

Canned Soups – Cream of celery and cream of mushroom are used in recipes as shortcuts and as flavorings or sauces; keep a few cans of them around. You probably also want to keep some cans of tomato or whatever your favorite is for eating when you don't want to make one from scratch.

Eggs – Eggs are very reasonably priced now. They're a good source of protein, Omega-3s, several other nutrients, and are used in most kinds of baked goods.

Milk – I like to use whole milk, but it comes in skim, 1%, and 2%. It tends to vary widely in price – right now it's very cheap. Sometimes it's more. I keep a couple cans of evaporated milk in my pantry; I use it if I run out of fresh, and it's saved me in a pinch. While it will taste different, you can reconstitute it for using on cereal, and straight, it's an adequate creamer for coffee or tea. You can use it in some recipes that call for cream – it's one of the options in the mix-and-match pumpkin pie recipe later, and would be fine in a soup or sauce. Condensed milk is different, and extremely sweet; it is useful in some dessert recipes, and in one way of preparing iced coffee in the summer. Dried milk is also handy; I'll add it to bread or pancakes sometimes.

Cheese – Cheese is not the cheapest thing on the list, but is delicious and good source of protein. It's often on sale; you can freeze cheese that you're going to use for cooking. This does change the texture, so you might not want to freeze what you'll use for sandwiches or just to eat. I keep cream cheese and few kinds of block cheese and shredded on hand. Check the prices when you buy – sometimes the shredded is cheaper than block, and sometimes it the other way around. I don't use over processed cheese-like substances; they don't taste as good and are not that good for me.

Cream – I like to use heavy cream in several foods I make regularly, and half and half in my coffee. Heavy cream is great for making homemade whipped cream, fruit fools (a light dessert), or adding richness to sauces. If you use it, keep a little carton in your fridge. If not, skip this one, as heavy cream is one of the pricier dairy products.

Meat Substitutes – There are an increasingly wide variety of these available, and prices have come down a bit. There are sandwich slices, burgers, non-chicken nuggets, even roasts. They are made from plant proteins. Some are vegan, some include eggs or dairy. Look for good sales of the ones that you like, and stock up then. They are highly processed, use accordingly.

Seasonings

A large part of ending up with delicious food after cooking is in the seasoning. The right seasonings make a cheap dinner taste better than a more costly, bland dinner. Imagine potatoes with no salt, or an apple pie without cinnamon. Edible, but lacking something.

Keeping a supply of the seasonings you use most is an integral part of cooking. At the same time, it's not something you can stock up on in huge amounts; over time, many seasonings start to lose flavor. If you get the extra-large jar of something that's on sale and cheaper than the small, but you don't use it up, after a few months, it will not have much flavor and you may as well throw it away. This is one reason to taste as you cook – if your spices are older, you may need to add more for the same effect.

There are a lot of possible seasonings, and I won't include all of them here. I'll discuss the ones that will be most used in the recipes in this book, and that are usually found at a reasonable price.

Herbs and spices both come from plants; the difference is what part of the plant was used. Herbs are from the leafy, green part of the plant. Spices are from any other part: seeds, bark, roots, bulb, stems. Sometimes both can be gotten from the same plant; the leaves of one particular plant are cilantro, while the seeds are coriander.

You can find herbs and spices in many stores, at widely varying prices. Sometimes the pricier ones are actually worth the extra, and sometimes the dollar bottle is just as good as the higher priced jar of the same. You can often find inexpensive spices at dollar stores or bent and dents. Some seasonings can be expensive, like saffron and whole vanilla beans, but I won't be listing them here; they're out of budget for most of what I cook.

Herbs

Herbs add seasoning to dishes, are often high in nutritional value, and frequently have both culinary and medicinal uses.

For herbs, there are two ways to use them – fresh or dried. You can substitute fresh for dried and vice-versa in most recipes. Typically, if a recipe calls for a tablespoon of a fresh herb, you'll use 1 tsp (1/3 T) in the recipe. Drying concentrates and shrinks the herbs. There are some recipes this won't work as well for; I made an intense herbal pasta sauce that wanted 3 cups of fresh basil, and put in one cup of dried. It tasted fine, but was a dull color and the texture was odd. Be sure to consider your particular recipe, and whether the substitutions will work for you in it.

Some of the herbs you will use the most often include:

Basil – If you look at the herb section of a nursery, there are a lot of varieties of basil, each slightly different. I usually end of getting a few different kinds, because they are so different looking and smell amazing. There are only a few types that are available dried in the seasoning section of stores, though. Basil is used in Mediterranean and Italian cooking. It tastes great on pizza, in soups, added to pastas, in sauces. It's one of the herbs I use most. I find myself in the summer looking at my several basil plants and urging them to grow so that I can pick them again.

Bay Leaves – These leaves are picked off of an evergreen shrub (or tree, depending on climate). It's also called laurel, and is the plant that was used to make victory wreaths in ancient Rome. Unlike other herbs, you usually remove the bay leaves after they've steeped enough for their flavor to permeate the dish. Bay leaves don't soften up – they're an evergreen, like a pine tree, only much better tasting – and can be physically sharp and unpleasant feeling. However, the flavor is amazing in soups, stews, marinades, and the like. I always put bay leaves in when I'm making lentil soups. Sometimes you use ground bay leaves, which stay in the food. Some recipes that use other herbs also use the steep-and-remove method of adding flavor.)

Chives – Chives are an allium, a relative of onions. They have a mild onion-like flavor. Instead of using the bulbs, you cut off and use their green tops. I have a window box of them that has been coming back every spring for years; they're one of the first herbs that are usable in spring and the last to die down in the fall.

Cilantro – Cilantro has the unusual trait that, while a majority of people will find it delicious, something like 12-20% of people have a genetic quirk (it's found on chromosome 11) that makes them think it tastes like dirt or soap. This trait is more common in people of European ancestry. So taste a bit, and see if you are in the, "wow, this is great!" or the, "ew, are you playing a trick on me?" group. Cilantro is used in recipes from a wide variety of places. It's popular in burritos or cooked with rice, in chili, stir-fries, soups, and dips. It's usually added right at the end as the recipe is completed, as cooking too long can reduce the flavor.

Dill – Dill is both herb and spice; you can use leaves, flowers, and seeds. The seeds are the part that stores best; dried leaves lose a lot of their flavor. Dill is used for making pickles, adding to soups, and making herbal butters and cheese.

Lemon Grass – Lemongrass is used in Asian cooking, tossed in a curry, soup, or stir-fry. It can be dried, ground, or used fresh. It has a subtle citrus flavor. It also makes a tasty herbal tea. I have it in my herbal tea collection, both on it's own and as part of several blends, and have a tube of lemongrass paste in my fridge for cooking.

Mints – There are a wide variety of mint plants – peppermint, spearmint, catnip, pennyroyal, apple mint, chocolate mint – at least 18 kinds, and then there are various hybrids and cultivars too. Mint is used to flavor desserts, drinks, and in candy. It can also be nice to just chew on a sprig of mint; it makes your breath tastes good and moistens your mouth if you're a bit thirsty. Some varieties of the mint family, like pennyroyal, are used most for non-culinary uses – pennyroyal might repel fleas, and makes a good ground cover.

Oregano – Oregano is used in wide variety of recipes, especially Italian and Greek, as well as having some medicinal properties. You can chew fresh leaves to lessen toothache, or throw a handful into a bath for additional relaxation. It's great in pasta sauces, herb butters, with tomatoes, with eggs, in herbed breads, or with pizza. It's easy to grow (bright sun, good drainage, water if you don't get enough rain) and sturdy.

Parsley – This is one of the most basic seasonings, found in dishes from all over the world. A lot of times people in the US think of it as just a garnish, but it has a many more uses than that. Parsley is used a lot in Middle Eastern cooking, being one of the main ingredients in salads instead of just an accent. I use it in gravies, chopped into sauces, in eggs, in herbed butters, in pastas, and just to chew on fresh.

Rosemary – Rosemary is an aromatic, almost bush-like plant. It makes a good potted herb to keep – while it won't winter over in temperate climates, a sunny window will keep it happy inside. In warm places, it can grow up into a ten foot tall bush. It smells great. It's used in Mediterranean cooking and in baked dishes. I like to toss root vegetables with olive oil, rosemary, and garlic and bake them.

Sage – Sage is used in a wide variety of dishes; it's good with squash, potatoes, soups, and gravies. It's a hardy plant. Of note is that sage is used in traditional ceremonies in several cultures, and is used in traditional medicinals as well.

Tarragon – Tarragon is much used in French cooking, often in conjunction with chives, parsley, and chervil in a blend called *aux fine herbes*. There are two kinds of tarragon, French and Russian. French has a more delicate flavor, but Russian is hardier to grow. I find this herb is absolutely delicious just chopped and scrambled with eggs in the morning.

Thyme – Thyme is has a strong scent and flavor, and is often used in savory dishes. It's often used with beans or tomatoes, and is the main ingredient in *boquet garni* and *herbs de Provence,* two of the primary French herbal blends. It's excellent with eggs, so is a good addition to omelets.

Spices

In European culture, spices were once incredibly exotic, expensive items brought at great cost and risk from unimaginably far lands. In medieval times wealthy people would sometimes just display their spices as a demonstration of wealth. A few peppercorns could cost weeks of an average European workingman's wages.

Now, most of them can be found at reasonable prices in almost any store that sells food.

Allspice – Allspice is the dried, ground berries of a tree that comes from Mexico/Central America. It's used a lot in Caribbean cooking and some Middle Eastern cooking as part of savory dishes. In the US and parts of Europe, it's mostly used in desserts – it's part of many pumpkin pie spice blends, cookies, and cakes.

Cardamom – This spice comes from India, and is the seeds of several related bushes. It's used in Indian cooking (obviously), and in cooking throughout Asia and the Middle East. In Nordic countries, it's used in baking bread and sweets.

Cinnamon – Cinnamon is made from the bark of several related trees. There are a couple of varieties of cinnamon available, but the least expensive, most readily available, and strongest flavored one is cassia. It's the one you think of when you think of cinnamon rolls, cinnamon sticks, or cinnamon cereals. The one that costs most, is hardest to get, and has the most delicate flavor is Ceylon.

Citrus – This can be a regular food, but parts of citrus fruit are often used as flavorings in recipes. Lemon juice, lemon zest (the finely grated outer peel), lime juice and zest, orange juice and zest are all used in recipes as seasonings.

Cloves – Cloves are the dried flower buds of a tree that comes from Indonesia. Their distinct flavor has made them popular in cooking all around the globe. Cloves are used in sweet and savory cooking, in drinks, in main dishes, side dishes, and desserts. They can be used whole (in which case you fish them out after the flavor has steeped into your dish, because they are hard and don't soften) or ground.

Coriander – This is the seeds of plant that is also called cilantro; usually when you use cilantro, you're talking about the leaves, and coriander is the seeds of the same plant.

Cumin – Cumin is the seed of a plant that originates in the Mediterranean area, but has been used as a spice for millennia. Ancient Greeks, Romans, Indians, Persians all used it. Cumin is in traditional recipes from all over the world. It's used in spice blends from chili powder to curry powder, and can be used ground or whole.

Garlic – Garlic is another allium (relative to onions). You usually use the root, called a bulb. The bulb is made up of many smaller pieces held together tightly; these are called cloves. (You can also use the pods of small garlics that grow up as the way they seed; you are unlikely to find this in a store, but can use them if you are growing your own garlic.) To use a fresh garlic clove, snap it off the bulb. Cut off the small, hard place where it was connected, and remove the papery covering. Then crush, chop, dice, slice, or use cloves whole, as your dish requires.

I find there is a significant difference in flavor between dried and fresh in this spice, though I will use whichever I have at hand. Dried is a bit sharper, and fresh more mellow, especially if you roast it first. You can also effect they flavor through different preparations of this before you put it in your dish; if you sauté it, it mellows even more (this isn't an option with dried garlic). You can bake it and mash it into recipes.

Ginger – Ginger a rhizome (sort of midway between a bulb and a root). It can be used dry and ground, or fresh and chopped, sliced, mashed, or candied, or crystallized. This is another spice where dried or fresh makes a big difference. Dry ginger is far stronger and spicier in taste; it tolerates higher temperatures and spreads quickly through a dish. Fresh ginger is mellower, spicy but with more complex flavors. It slowly infuses your dish, and the aromatic oils don't tolerate high or prolonged heat well. You can't really substitute them for each other, but if you must, use 1/8 to ½ tsp dried ginger for a tablespoon of fresh ginger. Ginger also has a lot of medicinal uses; the most well known is to settle an upset stomach.

Hot Peppers – There are a wide range of hot peppers out there. Researchers are constantly trying to rev it up and make spicier ones; the hottest ones out there come with warning labels – you won't usually find yourself cooking with those. The spiciness of a pepper is measured in Scoville units. You will probably keep a few different types of spicy peppers in your spice collection; paprika, cayenne, red pepper flakes, smoked paprika, or others at whatever level of heat you prefer.

Mace – Mace and nutmeg are closely related – nutmeg is the seed of a tree, and mace is the seed covering. Mace has a more delicate flavor than nutmeg, and is often used in baking, in soups, and in sauces.

Nutmeg – Nutmeg is used powdered; the actual nutmeg seeds are about the size of an acorn. It's used in recipes both sweet and savory, from eggnog to pastries to potatoes and soups. You can buy whole nutmeg and grate them yourself; this ensures the strongest flavor. It's also kind of a pain if you don't have a spice grinder; I'd suggest just getting pre-ground.

Peppercorns – These are not related to green peppers or hot peppers. Peppercorns are actually the dried seeds of a vine. The same plant produces black peppercorns, green peppercorns, and white peppercorns, depending on when it is picked and how it is prepared afterwards.

Turmeric – This spice is often used in Indian, Middle Eastern, and African cooking. It colors the food it's been used in a bright yellow. There is some research showing that turmeric might have some interesting health benefits.

Premade Blends

You might decide to keep several premade spice blends. It's a matter of preference; sometimes you just want to grab the can of pumpkin pie spice instead of grabbing separate containers of cinnamon, ginger, nutmeg, allspice, and cloves and measuring each of those out. I have a few mixes I just shake on when I don't want to get elaborate: pizza seasoning, Caribbean jerk, Mrs. Dash's, curry powder, and chili powder.

Another thing to consider is making your own blends. For instance, you can buy garlic salt, or you can mix a little garlic powder and dried parsley in some salt. Check prices; it may be cheaper. Making your own cinnamon sugar is definitely cheaper than buying the small bottles in the spice section of the store.

Salt

Salt is a mineral, rather than an herb or spice. It's one of the most basic food seasonings. You'll use it in most dishes. Be sure you have iodized salt; iodine is a necessary nutrient that's hard to get if you're not eating a lot of seaweed. If you're low on iodine, it will cause you thyroid problems.

Salt is also an important part of nutrition. Too much can cause issues like kidney stones or high blood pressure, and if you eat a lot of highly processed foods, fast food, or junk food, you may need to work on lowering your salt intake by eating more healthfully. But if you don't eat enough salt, or sweat the salt out, due to heat or exercise, and don't consume enough to replace it, that also has health consequences. If the sodium concentration in your blood gets too low, you can have mental confusion, dizziness, nausea, cramps, lethargy, and seizures. (The more severe symptoms are if you get very low on sodium.)

There are specialty salts available – sea salt, Hawaiian salt, Himalayan salt, and so on. They're not necessary, but you can try them if you want.

Keeping Your Food Costs Down

Knowing where and how to shop can make a big difference in how much groceries cost. There are a lot of tips that can help you keep expenses down.

Look for Sales and Coupons

Keep track of how much foods that you often use usually cost, and when they are on sale, get them then. Be sure that the stores not using the trick of claiming higher prices and pretending sales to make it look like the normal price is a sale price. Be careful about buying things you would not normally buy just because they are on sale. You can allot some of you budget to 'new foods' or 'things that are usually too costly', but keep the amount you budgeted.

You can also use coupons to bring down costs on some items. Be sure you are using them on things you would get otherwise; don't fall into the trap of buying it because you have a coupon instead of because it's something you need.

Discount Grocery Stores

See what different stores there are in your area, and go to the cheaper one. There are several discount grocery chains – the one near where I live is Aldi's, and it's only slightly farther to Sav-a-lot. These are distinctly less expensive on a lot of things than the more prominent grocery chains, so it's often a good starting point for shopping. Then go to the overall higher cost store for the few things the cheaper stores don't have.

You can also check bargain stores, like dollar stores, or odd lots stores, resale stores, and so on. They won't have a full range of groceries, but what they do have will be cheap. This will usually be packaged foods and nonperishables. You can get coffee, flour, pasta, canned fruit, and other staples. Keep in mind that these are only cheaper on some foods; dairy products, frozen and refrigerated goods, and produce usually cost more at these stores. They also tend to price a lot higher if they are the only store that carries food in the nearby area; if potential customers don't have other choices, they don't have to price competitively.

Comparison Shop

Compare prices between different sources; sometimes there can be significant differences. If stores in your area have weekly ads, see what's on sale at different stores. There are a lot of stores that carry some groceries, even if they are not focused on that. You might find that pasta costs less at a dollar store than it does at the regular grocery. There are also farmer's markets, orchards, a locally-sourced shop that has food (along with other locally-made things), and various people who sell the overflow from their gardens. These are all places that can have better prices – and in the case of the farmer's markets, better quality – foods.

Compare prices between brand names and generic. Often these things are of equal quality and taste, but the prices can be very different.

Bent and Dents

There may or may not be these where you live. It is definitely worth finding out. A bent and dent is a store that gets almost or just-expired foods, dinged up cans, overstocked, or less-popular groceries by the pound, and sells them at a serious discount. There are several in the county I live in; and they are really cost-effective ways of getting food. You have to be sure to check the cans and containers to be sure they are safe, but it usually is and it's cheap. For instance, coffee here is 9-11$ a bag at Kroger, 5-6$ at Aldi's, and $1.25 at the bent and dent. Canned goods are often a quarter a can. I can get a week's worth of groceries for the cost of a couple bags at a regular store.

You'll need to get familiar with your local store to see what it's specialties and focuses are. Then you'll have a good idea what you can get there, and what you'll need to look for in the other places we've talked about. There are two bent and dents in this county that I go to sometimes. The closest one has seasonal vegetables and fruits that the Amish proprietors grow in their garden or get from neighbors to sell. It's fresh and not expensive, but a very narrow selection. They also usually have a good selection of base ingredients like flour, oil, and spices, and a wide selection of coffees. The other one never has any fresh vegetables or fruit, but does get bread from a major outlet and has very good bread for a very cheap price, and often gets in higher quality candies than the first (Think Lindt truffles vs. Hershey's).

There are a few drawbacks. You have to be more careful to check quality. I've had a can of Pringles that had gone rancid that I had to throw away, and I've seen cans that didn't look good that I just left there. The stock is also unpredictable. They get their food by the pound from a distributor, and don't get a lot of choice as to exactly what they get in their flats of food. They will have pasta, but you don't know whether it will be spaghetti or macaroni. They will have canned vegetables, but whether it will be green beans or rutabagas is a toss-up. They often will not have much fresh food, though this varies depending on store.

Farmers' Markets, Orchards

Farmer's markets can be a great place to get fresh vegetables and fruits. They are where local food producers bring what they've grown. The food there tends to be local, seasonal, fresh, and flavorful. Most of it has not been picked slightly green and shipped, but has been picked perfectly ripe and brought over. The farmers might be local people who just sell the extra from their kitchen garden or larger food producers. There are some farmers who focus on making the most out of somewhat smaller acreages, and selling their produce at farmers markets, local restaurants, or gourmet groceries.

As far as costs, you'll need to check and compare; in some areas, the farmer's markets cost more than grocery stores, and in others, they are much less. It depends a bit on what the food is – peaches from the farmer's market here, in season, are cheaper, while berries (picked by locals) are more, due to costs of labor.

If you want to make apple sauce, jam, freeze foods, can, or otherwise stock up, you will want to check orchards or u-picks for prices. It can be a lot less expensive to buy a bushel of apples at an orchard than it is to buy half a dozen bags of them at a grocery store, and they will be fresher and better quality for your preserves. If this is what you want to do, check prices at a few. There is one orchard nearby that sells what is called seconds for cooking and preserving; they cost a third what apples do even at the other orchards, and there's nothing wrong with that apples except that they aren't pretty – they may have an uneven color or be a funny shape, but they taste fine and make delicious sauce, butter, and pie.

Gardening

Another way to get food is to grow your own. Even if you only keep pots of favorite herbs on a windowsill, it will add something to your cooking, and be something that you don't have to buy.

Growing your own food is a great way to help you make sure you have the freshest, tastiest food possible. Gardening also is excellent exercise. Depending on what you grow, you can also significantly decrease your food expenditures. Think about what vegetables and fruits you eat the most of, how much space you have available, how much time you have available, and how much prep work you are willing to do. I'm not going to include a lot about how to grow; that would (and might yet) be its own book. This will just include some things to keep in mind.

Two tomato plants, well-tended, will enable you to eat fresh tomatoes all summer (You will need two, unless your neighbor is also growing them so that they'll be able to pollinate each other) A few more, and some time, work, and storage containers, and you can freeze, can, or dry enough to last you over the winter and spring until more plants grow. A few more, and maybe you can sell garden-fresh tomatoes, or put up your own tomato paste, spaghetti sauce, or pizza sauce. But if you don't eat many tomatoes, you're probably better off just buying a couple on the times when you do want one.

Some food, while you can grow it, may be too much work for a home gardener. While you *could* grow your own wheat, it would take a lot of space, effort, and equipment to grow and process enough to make your own flour. It's simpler and more cost effective to buy it. Some things, like beans, you'll need to consider. They're easy to grow, and freezing or canning green beans is not difficult. It's more work to process and store dried beans, but still possible; you'll need to decide if it's better for you to grow or buy foods like that.

Think about your favorite recipes; maybe that will what you plan your garden around. A pasta sauce garden would include tomatoes, peppers, onions, garlic, and herbs.

Consider your budget too, when planning. A package of seeds is cheap; a 3-pack of 6 inch seedlings cost more, and single 18" plant even more. But maybe not having to spend two months babying up seeds to pepper plants that are large enough to plant in the garden means it's worth buying already started plants. I usually do a split; lettuce grows quickly and easily enough I can spend a dollar on seeds, plant them in the spring, and have them for a while. Eggplants take weeks to get large and hardy enough to set out, and I don't eat a lot of them, so I just buy a couple plants at the greenhouse.

Don't let not having a yard stop you from growing food if you want to. Many communities have community garden spaces that are shared, either freely, for rent, or for barter. And you can grow food plants indoors too.

Indoor plants are proven to improve mood and mindset, increase your sense of well-being, purify the air indoors (up to 87 percent of air toxins within a day or two), and decrease background noise. Because they are so connected to well-being, most people have at least some houseplants. Even if you live in a small apartment, you can grow some fresh herbs, or even some food plants. Instead of a merely decorative plant, consider a pot of lettuce, or several fresh herbs on the windowsill of your kitchen. This also means that you can have some fresh foods, even in winter, if you choose well and have good lighting.

Seasonal Produce

When you hear people talk about seasonal produce, they are talking about the fresh fruits and vegetables that are ripe at that time of the year. This varies by region. With modern shipping methods, we can have almost any food at any time. However, that has drawbacks. Shipping food that far constantly has a large carbon footprint. Food is often picked slightly less than ripe, so that it will ripen on arrival; this means it may not be as flavorful. And farmers growing food for shipping have to select hardy, shippable varieties; these often are not the best-tasting. Some of the more flavorful varieties of foods don't ship well at all.

You also have more choices with seasonal foods. They are usually locally grown, and some of the delicate varieties that don't ship well are available. Again consider strawberries; the ones that come from California or Mexico up to Maine or Ohio in December have to be very firm, so that they don't bruise and spoil. This comes at a cost to some flavor. Berries picked locally in June or July will be softer, a little tender, and (I find) twice as fragrant and flavorful.

The fruits and vegetables that are in season will often (though not always) be the least expensive. For instance, asparagus costs a lot more in winter than it does in spring.

What's in season will vary a lot depending on where you are located. Right now, it's November and I'm in Ohio. What's in season is cabbages, apples, winter squash, cruciform vegetables, root vegetables, and some herbs. If it was June, it would be lettuce, strawberries, blueberries, corn, green beans, peas, cucumbers, rhubarb, summer squash, and herbs.

You can find what's in season in your area using websites like www.seasonalfoodguide.org, in a farmer's almanac, with a visit to the local farmer's market, or in a gardening book.

Strategic Cooking

Planning ahead is a big part of keeping your food budget in line. If you get home from work or errands, hungry, tired, and grumpy, and try to figure out what you are going to make, chances are it's going to be fatty, sweet, and fast, as that's what bodies crave in those conditions; our bodies instinctively feel, "there is no food and what will we do we're going to starve quick get the most energy possible fast!" This makes impulse buys and fast-food grabbing big temptations.

Planning doesn't automatically lead to tons of work, take all the fun out of cooking, no creativity or spontaneity. While it can mean making up a months' worth of casseroles and freezing them, that's more than you have to do. Planning is simply being aware of what your values are as far as food, and lining up your actions to match.

Planning means you know what's there – you're not feeling overwhelmed trying to choose. You don't stand in front of the fridge blankly trying to figure out what's for dinner, then just think, "forget it, I'm ordering pizza", or grab a bag of chips to "snack" on and find you've eaten all of them. (Not that you never get pizza, or eat chips, but plan it or set a limit so you don't get in an unhealthy rut.)

Planning means you know what you need to buy. You might have a list, and you aren't just impulsively tossing things into your cart. This saves a lot of money. You can plan a certain amount each week for impulse buying groceries; this gives you both choices and is a part of your planned budget, so you don't run out of money.

Planning might mean you get some preparation done ahead of time. Start the beans in the slow cooker in the morning so they're ready when you get home from work. Bake the cake earlier so it's ready for dinner. If you know it's a busy day the next day, chop up some ingredients and stick them in the fridge so it's easy when you're cooking later.

Planning means less waste. You know there's leftover mashed potatoes, so you plan to use them up before they go bad and make colcannon the next day. Or there are beans, so now you have burritos for lunch. Or there is too much cornbread, so you freeze some for later. This saves time and money – you have things prepared so you don't have to start from nothing, and you have to buy less because you are using more of it.

Part of thrifty preparation includes being able to use up all of what you've bought or prepared. If you have a large family, it's not that hard to use up an entire head of cabbage, or a whole pot of cooked beans. But if you're cooking for just a few or one, you'll need to be creative.

It's possible to prepare one main ingredient or food and use that for a variety of dishes. For instance, beans. You can cook up a slow cooker or pan of dried beans. You can then have cornbread and beans for dinner, burritos for lunch, bean burgers for a meal, or bean soup for another dinner. This doesn't have to all be in a row; they're good for a week, so you can skip a day. Or freeze them for a long time later; but make use of it, and do so in a way that cuts down your work and makes the most of cheap ingredients. Lentils are another great one for this; prepare a pot of lentils, then make lentil burgers, lentil soup, lentil loaf, and lentil curry. You can buy cabbage when it's on sale, and have baked cabbage steaks, sautéed cabbage side, colcannon bake, and add it to a soup, stew, or potpie. Think about how your ingredients are going to fit together; you'll have less go to waste.

What if your planning doesn't go quite right? Sometimes you will think you have an ingredient, start the recipe, and discover that no, in fact you do not have baking powder, or eggs, or sour cream. That doesn't mean you've just wasted ingredients, or, if you were smart and checked before starting, that you have to change your plans and make something else. You can often make some substitutions.

You can also make substitutions to make some recipes vegan or vegetarian, or to avoid a food sensitivity, or to make it healthier.

Substitutions

If you're out of baking powder, use 1/4 the amount of baking soda and something a little acidic to balance it out. It only needs to be a little acidic – even applesauce will do it. Buttermilk, a few drops of lemon juice, yogurt, molasses, coffee, a few drops of vinegar, cream of tartar, whichever best matches your recipe.

If you're substituting dried herbs for fresh, or vice versa, think a 1 to 3 ratio – use 1/3 the amount of dried herbs as were called for with fresh, or use 3 times the amount of fresh herbs for the needed amount of dry. Example – a recipe calls for 1/4 cup of fresh chopped parsley. You do not have fresh parsley. A third of 1/4 cup is 1 1/3 tablespoons, so you use 1 1/3 tablespoons of dried parsley instead.

Spices are different, *do not* use the 1:3 ratio with them. You'll have to look up the particular spice you are trying to convert. They are all different – 1 tablespoon of fresh ginger is equivalent to 1/8 teaspoon of dried, for instance, while 1 clove of fresh garlic is 1/3 tsp dried. As noted in the spice section, these conversions may change the flavor.

You can substitute plain yogurt for sour cream in most recipes, and vice versa.

There are a few ways to substitute things for eggs in baking recipes. Ground flax seed, when mixed with fluids, puts out a slimy kind of goo that makes it a great substitute for eggs in many baking recipes. Whisk 1 T of finely ground flax seed with 3 T of water for each egg you are replacing. Flax seed makes brown flecks and has a nutty taste, so consider that when you're changing up your recipe. It's a good egg substitute in banana, zucchini, and other quick breads, in brownies, and in pancakes. You'd have to experiment and see what it does for your other cake recipes, and it won't work if you are trying to use it instead of egg white for a meringue or recipe that uses beaten egg whites as a source of leavening.

You can often substitute a mashed banana or applesauce for half (or even a bit more) of the oil in quick bread recipes.

Glossary

AL DENTE: Italian term used to describe pasta that is cooked until it offers a slight resistance when you bite it.

BAKE: To cook by dry heat, usually in the oven. You can bake things in a crockpot, breadmaker, or fire.

BASTE: To moisten foods during cooking with pan drippings or special sauce to add flavor and prevent drying.

BATTER: A mixture containing flour and liquid, thin enough to pour.

BEAT: To mix rapidly in order to make a mixture smooth and light by incorporating as much air as possible.

BLANCH: To immerse in rapidly boiling water and allow to cook slightly, preserving the color and vitamins. Used to help make peeling peaches and tomatoes easier.

BLEND: To incorporate two or more ingredients thoroughly.

BOIL: To heat a liquid until bubbles break continually on the surface.

BROIL: To cook on a grill under strong, direct heat.

CARAMELIZE: To heat sugar in order to turn it brown and give it a special taste.

CHOP: Cut food into similarly-sized pieces; these pieces can be larger (coarsely chopped) or tiny (finely chopped)

CONCHE: A conche is a surface scraping mixer and agitator that evenly distributes cocoa butter within chocolate, and may act as a "polisher" of the particles. Good chocolate is conched for a long while to even out the texture.

CLARIFY: To separate and remove solids from a liquid, thus making it clear.

CREAM: When not referring to the dairy product, but the cooking technique, it means to soften a fat, especially butter, by beating it at room temperature. Butter and sugar are often creamed together, making a smooth, soft paste.

DICE: To cut food in small cubes of uniform size and shape.

DREDGE: To coat with flour or other fine substance. Usually done by carefully rolling or turning the food to be dredged in flour, crumbs, etc.

DUST: To sprinkle food with dry ingredients. Use a strainer or a jar with a perforated cover, or try the good, old-fashioned way of shaking things together in a paper bag.

Fines Herbes: Traditional spice blend in French cooking: often parsley, chives, tarragon, chervil. Used in delicate dishes, eggs, sauces. (Any of these are delicious scrambled up in eggs.)

FOLD: To incorporate a delicate substance, such as whipped cream or beaten egg whites, into another substance without releasing air bubbles. Gently cut down through mixture with spoon, whisk, or fork; go across bottom of bowl, up and over, close to surface. The process is repeated, while slowing rotating the bowl, until the ingredients are thoroughly blended.

FRY: To cook in hot oil. To cook in a small amount of oil is called pan-frying or sautéing; to cook in a one-to-two inch layer of hot oil is called shallow frying; to cook in a deep layer of hot oil is called deep frying.

herbs de Provence: Blend of dried herbs traditional to Provence area of France; usually marjoram, savory, rosemary, thyme, and oregano, sometimes other herbs added too.

JULIENNE: To cut vegetables, fruits, or cheeses into thin strips.

KNEAD: To work and press dough with the palms of the hands or mechanically, for instance, in a stand mixer with a dough hook, to develop the gluten in the flour.

LUKEWARM: Approximately body temperature.

MARINATE: To flavor and moisturize pieces of protein (tofu, seitan) or vegetable (useful for eggplants) by soaking them in or brushing them with a liquid mixture of seasonings known as a marinade.

MINCE: Chopping something very, very fine, often just by rocking a blade over it.

MIX: To combine ingredients usually by stirring..

PARE: To remove the outermost skin of a fruit or vegetable. This is where your paring knife gets its name; before potato peelers were invented, you used a small-bladed knife to peel things.

PEEL: To remove the peels from vegetables or fruits.

PLUMP: To soak dried fruits in liquid until they swell.

PUREE: To mash foods until perfectly smooth by hand, by rubbing through a sieve or food mill, or by whirling in a blender or food processor. You'll do this to applesauce, fruit butters, soups that you want to have smooth, and sauces that are lumpier than you like.

REDUCE: To boil down to reduce the volume.

REFRESH: To run cold water over food that has been parboiled, to stop the cooking process quickly. Technically what you call it when you dunk your just-blanched peaches into the ice water.

ROAST: To cook by dry heat in an oven in an open pan – no lid or tinfoil.

ROUX: a mixture of fat (especially butter) and flour used in making sauces. Blending fat and flour over heat makes the flour more effective in thickening sauces. It's also tasty. You can cook the roux for different times; cooking until it's tan or light brown (be careful not to burn) leads to a nice, nutty flavor.

SAUTE: Cooking food quickly over high heat, usually in oil or another fat, like butter.

SEAR: Cook an ingredient over very high heat for a brief period of time; the food is not moved until it has become fully browned.

SIMMER: Cook in a liquid that is just below the boiling point, between 180 and 205 degrees. You should see bubbles forming, but they should be gentle and not at a full roll. If a food needs simmering, watch carefully that it doesn't fully boil – that means it's too hot.

STEAM: To cook with boiling water, although the ingredients never touch the water itself. By placing a steamer basket above boiling water, the ingredient cooks at 212 degrees without losing any of its flavor to the water. You'll often use this to cook vegetables or cabbage rolls.

SCALD: To bring to a temperature just below the boiling point, usually then removing from heat. Often refers to cooking with milk.

SIFT: To put one or more dry ingredients through a sieve or sifter.

SKIM: To remove impurities, whether scum or fat, from the surface of a liquid during cooking, thereby resulting in a clear, cleaner-tasting final produce. For instance, rice and beans often make foam on top of the water when cooking. This isn't bad or dirty, but I usually skim it off because I find it unsightly.

SLICE: Cut large ingredients or foods into similarly shaped, flat pieces; for instance, slicing bread, or slicing a potato into disks.

STEEP: To extract color, flavor, or other qualities from a substance by leaving it in water just below the boiling point.

STERILIZE: To destroy microorganisms by boiling, dry heat, or steam. The heat helps slow or prevent spoiling; for instance, if you are going to try canning you fruit butter, you'll sterilize the jars before you put any food in them.

STEW: To simmer slowly in a small amount of liquid for a long time.

STIR: To mix ingredients with a circular motion until well blended or of uniform consistency.

TOSS: To combine ingredients with a lifting motion.

WHIP: To beat rapidly to incorporate air and produce expansion. You'll used this with eggs and cream most often. I've seen people use the liquid off a can of chickpeas to make a kind of vegan whipped cream; that takes a lot of whipping. This is much easier with an electric mixer.

Thank you so much for buying *Vegetarian Cooking on a Budget*! I hope you've found something that made you think, "That sounds delicious!", and that you have fun experimenting in your kitchen.

If you liked my book, learned from it, found it useful, or have a suggestion, please put a review on Amazon for me.

I hope have as much fun reading this book as I have had in writing it for you!

I love to hear from my readers, ideas, thoughts, or questions. Contact me at:

www.writeuseful.com

or thewritingone@outlook.com

or Write Useful on Facebook

Watch for the next book in the Living on a Budget series, *Maintaining a Household on a Budget.*

We'll talk about everything you need to know to set up housekeeping and maintain your own home.

While waiting, enjoy the following sample of another book in the series, *Sewing on a Budget,* available in paperback on Amazon and on Kindle.

First Chapter from *Sewing on a Budget*

Why Sew?

Why bother doing your own sewing? What use is sewing in modern life, when you can locate whatever you want in a store or online? And isn't it pricey?

Get Exactly What You Want

I have a terrible time finding clothes that fit my chest and hips. Button up anything, and it either gaps indecently or hangs on the rest of me like a gunnysack. My husband often finds that ready-made pants bought in the store are too long. It can be difficult to get clothes that fit you well and look nice; I suspect you and your friends have many stories about the challenges of finding well-fitting off the rack clothes. And when you add in any personal tastes that might not be what stores are carrying now, it becomes even more difficult.

But you have control of your clothing when you sew. You can make sure your clothes fit – this is really significant. With sewing, I can either buy clothes that are a little big and fit around those excessive attributes, then alter them down so that the entire garment fits. I can do a full bust adjustment on a pattern and make one that fits me perfectly from the get-go. You can page through pattern books and find a much wider variety of clothes than are available in stores; and when you add finding them online or in thrift shops, you have even more choices available.

I can make clothes in colors and patterns that I like, rather than being limited to whatever the manufacturers have decided is "in" this season. A few years ago, everything was neon or chartreuse or orange. It was hideous. I thrifted and made clothes that I liked, rather than being stuck with what the stores in my small town had available.

When you sew, you have control over the materials used. Want organic clothing? Make your own. Source organic fabric and thread, and get what you want, in the styles you want. (Keep in mind that organic material is more expensive.) Need only soft fabrics due to sensitivities? Yours for the making. Want to use only retro fabric? Find it online, or get vintage fabric from second-hand stores.

If you have a style you want that is hard to find, make it. For instance, if you like vintage, you can find some old patterns – thrift stores are great for this, and the major pattern companies have a retro division now, reprinting a few from each decade – and make what you want. Steampunk, Goth, Lagenlook – what was once difficult to find or completely out of reach is possible when you can make whatever you want.

This isn't limited to clothes. I've had a terrible time finding curtains I like for some remodeling we're doing in our home. The ones in the store are bland and made of cheap, ugly fabric, or else ridiculously costly. I found a bolt of fabric at a yard sale that is almost the color I want (I might dye it a bit darker) and I'm going to make some pretty patchwork borders to sew along the bottom, and my new curtains will be exactly what I want, instead of what the store sees fit to offer. They'll go great with the patchwork quilts that are on the bed.

When I was young, my mother (and then I once I learned) made my own doll clothes; at first because the store-bought ones tore too easily, and then because I was reading a lot of old books like *Little Women* and *Little House on the Prairie*, and I wanted my dolls' clothes to match was I was reading. Still later, I learned to make dolls, stuffed animals, and dollhouse accessories to give to the children in my life. Well-made, age-appropriate, educational toys – especially if they're made with natural materials – tend to be priced astronomically high. One popular type of fabric doll "made from all-natural materials" is priced at over a hundred dollars just for the doll and one outfit. Another one I found while researching for this book was closer to forty dollars, but still, you can make a doll with an entire wardrobe and accessories for less than that.

Have exact control over what you wear, what you use, the toys available, how you decorate. It's all in your own hands and choices.

Less, or at least equitable, Cost

If you walk into an average fabric or crafting store, one thing you notice very quickly if you are on a tight budget is just how expensive things can be. It's very easy to think, "I'm going to save some money by sewing my own stuff", go in the store, find out how much all the bits and pieces for that dress cost, and walk right out again, discouraged. But it is possible to save money sewing, and to find what you need for less than this first glance would seem to show you. Sewing doesn't have to be high-priced.

One factor to keep in mind is, to what are you comparing the cost? I was at a store recently and they had summer dresses for $8. I thought, "I can't make it for that price" and bought half a dozen. The first time I washed one, the embroidery started coming loose, the fabric frayed, and some of the seams came undone. Turned out those inexpensive dresses were not actually lower cost or better value; they were just that, cheap, and weren't even worth what had looked like a good price. On the other hand, I have a summer work dress I made 8 years ago. I've raked hay on my parents' farm in that dress, I've done deep cleaning, heavy gardening, and animal care. It's been washed dozens and dozens of times, and is just now starting to wear thin. I have had to mend the pockets a couple times, and patch a tear that it got from snagging on a tool. But it's definitely been a better value than my one-wash-and-it's-over cheap dresses. And it wasn't exactly expensive to start with; I used modestly priced cotton fabric, thread, and some interfacing.

Compare the fabric quality (threads per inch, type of material, sturdiness) and the detail. Compare the fit, and consider what kind of sewing you are doing. If you are refashioning or altering up thrift store finds, it's going to be pretty inexpensive. You can often find fabric at thrift stores (more on that later). If you are using high-quality work (your own efforts, individually, will be of good quality – you keep at it till it's just right), detail, and materials when you create, compare that quality of garment to comparable store-bought clothing, not to the cheapest thing you can find. Choose your materials carefully, using some of the sources and ideas found in this book, and you'll find that the costs are at least equitable, will be a better value, and will more than likely even be cheaper.

Lengthen the Life of Your Fabric Belongings

Keeping your clothes in good shape by mending them instead of throwing them not only helps reduce waste, it saves you money you don't have to spend getting new clothes. Instead of tossing that shirt when it gets a stain, sew a decorative patch on it. Mend small tears before they become big ones – that's the source of the famous saying, "a stitch in time saves nine." Fix it when it's small, and save yourself a big job later. Thighs of your jeans getting thin? Darn them by hand or on machine, or stitch in internal patches. Pocket torn on your purse? Sew that tear back up, and keep on using it. Hem starting to fall out of your favorite dress? It's an easy fix. You don't have to buy and replace things as often when you are able to maintain them on your own.

I tend to dislike clothes shopping, so keeping my clothes in good shape means I can avoid that chore. My husband is hard on clothes; he tears them at work. He likes outdoor activities, and often comes back from fishing or hunting with tears. Mending cuts down on how often he's got to replace things (and keeps his favorite shirt in good shape.) If you've made an item, you know exactly how it goes together and can repair or replace any torn or stained areas.

Knowing how to sew, and having some tools around with which to do so, allows you to keep your things nice and in good condition for longer.

Creativity

Expressing your creativity is one of the major reasons you might want to sew. Even people who are not on a budget, trying to recycle, or choosy about what they want love to sew as a way to express themselves and feel the satisfaction of finishing something creative.

310

It's fun to plan out what you are making – what colors, patterns, styles. Making your one-of-a-kind clothes, toys, home decor, quilts, or decorations is amazingly enjoyable.

Even when people were sewing for necessity, because if they didn't they had no clothes or blankets, they found ways to express themselves and create beauty. Look through pictures of antique quilts; you can feel the creativity invested in making something both beautiful and thrifty, of not only making use of every scrap of material, but also making it lovely.

You can join this tradition of making the needful beautiful and fun. Imagine gazing out your window and thinking of how uninspired the blinds are; you start thinking about what you can do to make it different. You see different ideas and colors, and the next thing you know, you're sketching out a quick idea on the back of a receipt and thinking of what you have already, and what you need to get, to make your vision become a reality.

It takes creative thinking to search for the best bargains, to plan out the best ways to make use of that old curtain to make something new and better, to decide how to make the best memory item from a loved one's shirt.

Creativity has been woven throughout all the other answers. It takes creativity to look at an old 80's muumuu and see the possibilities hidden in it. You'll use creative thinking when you consider ways to use all the scraps and pieces of worn clothes and fabric items instead of just tossing them. It can take a lot of creative thinking to find the best way to mend that place where your sleeve caught on that gate.

All of the many things you can make are a chance to express yourself. Choose your colors, your materials, your purpose and bring your creative vision to light.

Environmental Responsibility

We hear a lot about the environment, reducing waste, and helping keep our world in good shape. Your sewing skills can help with this; sewing can definitely be environmentally responsible. Choose your sources of materials well. Use fabrics that have a lower environmental impact during manufacture, reuse older fabric items, repurpose scraps left from other projects, or buy mill-ends and end-of-bolts so they aren't thrown away. Mending is another one, but it has its own section.

A great way to lower your environmental impact (and keep costs down) is refashioning old or second hand clothes. This practice has been around forever; centuries ago, if father's clothes were worn, they'd use the good parts to make clothes for son. The lady of the house's old clothes would be given to the maid to make over for herself. Last season's dresses would be made up to look chic and new. This has not gone away. There are entire websites and YouTube channels that center around remaking – also called upcycling. I've seen some gorgeous remakes from thrift store finds. You can find a large shirt or dress, and use the fabric to make yourself something new, or simply make a few changes to an almost-perfect garment. This both prevents waste and is a source of very low-cost materials for you to work with.

Use scraps of old clothes to make quilts, rugs, bags. Even the leftovers from other projects can be used to cut down on what you send to the trash and to save money. Keep your fabric snips and thread ends; when you have enough, use them to stuff a pillow or a dog bed.

Use old sheets as a source for fabric. You can find high-quality sheets in good repair in many second-hand stores. Or, as your sheets wear out, don't toss them. Use the parts that are still good to make something. My bottom sheets always wear out before the top sheet, and a top sheet is yards of good, prewashed, preshrunk, soft material.

Use your creativity and craft to reduce your environmental impact and help save the planet.

Quality

Things you make yourself, once you get a little experience, are higher quality then most thing you can buy, except for things in the highest cost brackets. The fabrics you choose to use are better. The workmanship can be much more thorough and exacting (depending on your own efforts). The seams can be stronger, the detailing more exact. Hand-crafted items will last longer. Remember my summer dresses that weren't actually such a great find, and the handmade one that's lasted years? Handmade toys last longer than most inexpensive bought ones; I've still got the rabbit my Mom made for me when I was a toddler. He's been mended a lot, but he's in great shape.

You can choose better materials, and can make things in a more detailed and longer-lasting way. You control the quality when you are sewing for yourself.

Personal Satisfaction

Try this: close your eyes, imagine yourself holding up your finished project, knowing you made this, from ideas to choices of pattern, fabric, and decoration. You wrestled through the tricky bits. You learned a new technique to add that decorative item to the hem. You scratched yourself on a pin and had to find a way to get out a tiny bloodstain. And now it's done! You did it. you overcame all the obstacles and have a thing.

You've probably had this feeling when you've finished a tough assignment at work or school, or gotten a chore you've been dreading out of the way (cleaning the refrigerator? The basement?). Those things provide satisfaction when finished, but they aren't usually much fun while you're doing them. Sewing gives you both - enjoyment of the process, and pride when you finish the work.

What will you do with the thing you've created? Maybe it's a gift for your Dad's birthday, or for a baby shower. Perhaps you've signed up with a charity to make blankets for shelter dogs, or tiny clothes for stillborn babies, or teddy bears for kids being put into foster care. Maybe it's your new little black dress and you're going out with friends this weekend. Maybe it's a quilted cover for your bed, or a bag for your computer.

Whatever it is, you made it. It's yours; hold it, and enjoy the feeling of having created it.

And a final word...

I like this blessing, and I pass it to you.

May there always be work for your hands to do.
May your purse always hold a coin or two.
May the sun always shine upon your window pane.
May a rainbow be certain to follow each rain.
May the hand of a friend always be near to you and
May God fill your heart with gladness to cheer you.

And I will visit with you again in the next book in this series!